THE POLITICS OF SHAKESPEARE

The Politics of Shakespeare

Derek Cohen
Associate Professor of English
York University, Ontario

First published in Great Britain 1993 by
THE MACMILLAN PRESS LTD
Houndmills, Basingstoke, Hampshire RG21 2XS
and London
Companies and representatives
throughout the world

A catalogue record for this book is available
from the British Library.

ISBN 0–333–59886–5

Printed and bound in Great Britain by
Antony Rowe Ltd, Chippenham, Wiltshire

First published in the United States of America 1993 by
Scholarly and Reference Division,
ST. MARTIN'S PRESS, INC.,
175 Fifth Avenue,
New York, N.Y. 10010

ISBN 0–312–10187–2

Library of Congress Cataloging-in-Publication Data
Cohen, Derek.
The politics of Shakespeare / Derek Cohen.
p.   cm.
Includes index.
ISBN 0–312–10187–2
1. Shakespeare, William, 1564–1616—Political and social views.
2. Politics and literature—Great Britain—History—16th century.
3. Politics and literature—Great Britain—History—17th century.
4. Political plays, English—History and criticism.   I. Title.
PR3017.C59   1993
822.3'3—dc20   93–8141

10   9   8   7   6   5   4   3   2
04   03   02   01   00   99   98   97   96

Solemnly dedicated to the Shugarman Memorialists

Contents

Acknowledgements

I should like to thank the editors of the *University of Toronto Quarterly*, *Neophilologus* and *Modern Language Quarterly* for permission to include revised versions of essays which have found places in their journals. To my old friends, Harry Cohen, John Perry, Leon Rabinowitz, and Sandra and Steven Joffe, I offer thanks for wonderful hospitality. I once again acknowledge the sustaining presence of my children, Sam and Sophie, and, also, Eunjung. I am grateful to my parents, Barney and Anita Cohen, for their constant encouragement and support and for establishing an example of courageous political action and behaviour in the apartheid-ruled South Africa of the 1950s and 1960s. This book draws its political direction so heavily from my South African upbringing and experience that I feel some acknowledgement is due to the scattered comrades of the African Resistance Movement – ARM.

1
Introduction

In some senses the pivotal chapter in this book is that on *Measure for Measure* and the problem of classic liberalism. It is there that I attempt to explain some of the basic political assumptions of the book and to account for the failure that liberalism represents to me. The socialist bias of the book derives from active personal experience of liberalism and then socialism in the crucible of South African politics during the fifties and sixties. It seems to me that the reading of Shakespearean drama has historically been hedged with liberal assumptions which, though normally unstated, have limited the kinds of scrutiny to which the plays have been subjected. Those liberal limits have indeed been wide and it is this very width which is at once the glory and the weakness of the liberal agenda. Liberalism has exposed itself in the very breadth of interpretation to which the plays have been subjected, so that *Othello* has been used to confirm and deny the mythologies around racism, as *The Merchant of Venice* has been used to confirm and deny the dogmas of anti-Semitism. The list goes on. But, basically, its length and history derive from the assumption that the plays emanate from a culture whose political elasticity is able to accommodate only apparently opposite ideologies. Part of the reason for the evident malleability of Shakespeare's dramas is the fact of liberalism as a dominant force in Western cultures. Central to that ideology is the concept of individualism which has, arguably, been in the making for many centuries.[1] The critical celebration of the ambiguity of literature has always been predicated on a belief in liberal individualism. Schizophrenic drama like Shakespeare's, which can simultaneously contain multiguous meanings, depends upon the belief in an original unity; Liberal 'liberality' depends upon a belief in the unique wholeness of the individual subject and his limited freedom to act within the confines of that politics.

My discussion of *Measure for Measure* is an exploration of some of the ideological and historical facets of liberalism. It is an attempt to expose the ways in which liberalism and capitalism are mutually complicit, are interdependent and inextricable from each other, in

1

a text that, naturally, precedes the systematic codification of both ideologies, but which possesses the birthmarks of these integrally related ideological systems. The socialist alternative to capitalism, which has supplied the philosophical basis of much recent writing on Shakespeare has, to some extent, liberated the canon from the constraints of the liberal politics with which it has usually been informed. The relationship – potential or mythical – between socialism and liberalism has been the cause of some disagreement amongst political theorists and is given some attention in Chapter 8. While C. B. Macpherson, to give one leading example, sees a potential compatibility between socialism and liberalism,[2] other socialist theorists have until recently tended to deny the possibility of such linkage.

A socialist perspective implies a concentration on the inevitably adversarial relations of the classes which are represented and implicit in the plays. These relations, perceptible in Shakespeare's dramatic constructions of individual behaviour – deference, respect, and what we call good and bad manners – and intestine class warfare – such as that so egregiously conducted in *2 Henry VI* – are, obviously, relations of power. There are the classes which have and wish to keep power and those which, in every sense of the word, want power. The compatibility of these classes is one of the more potent of the liberal myths which is both contained in and exploded by the plays. And it is the fostering of that myth by liberalism and its precursor ideologies which has helped justify and maintain systematic class oppression for many centuries. It has recently become fashionable to equate the failure of Soviet and Soviet-style Communism with the failure of socialism itself and the invalidity of the socialist ideology, and to draw from this putative lesson a 'truth' about the fallacy of socialism entirely. The unfortunate result of such thinking has been a hard fall back into the arms of liberal capitalism as a demonstrably 'right' and 'true' dogma because it survived the very thing it was trying to bludgeon to death for a century. In short, Shakespeare studies have been affected by the collapse of the Berlin Wall. For, in the survival of capitalism and the destruction of Soviet hegemony, liberalism and liberal reading, without really having lost ground in the West,[3] have been revivified and re-empowered and, perhaps, more than before, cultural materialism needs to fight for air.

The chapters which follow take for granted the presence of a class struggle through history. Sometimes the signs of the struggle have been expunged, sometimes its sound has been stilled, but it is always there. The Western use, appropriation and celebration of individualism has had a profound impression on some of the forms which that struggle has taken. Shakespeare's plays were produced in a world which recognized that struggle, and they were given form by a system of cultures whose leaders sought to keep power out of the hands of the poor and the many partly through the validation of individualism and individual enterprise. Part I contains analyses of the relationship of society to its unassimilable individuals. These relationships, predictably, take the form of an oppressive politics of the suppression of such individuals – Othello, Shylock, and Caliban – as are located outside the society which acknowledges them only as strangers whose strangeness is confirmed by their physical difference. In their perceptions of society from that outside locus lies the source of much revealing political tension. Each of these individuals understands the fact that his survival depends upon resistance to the political domination to which all eventually succumb. In each case it is clear that the individual in question, though he seems alone in the Western, Christian world of the play, comes from a group or a people which actually or potentially threatens the Western, Christian order that dominates the politics of the drama. The hatred and fear expressed towards these individuals is clearly an anticipatory response to the population which each represents. Shylock's story supplies a study in the hatred of the stranger which united social loathing can engender. For Shylock, his own hatred becomes a weapon and a staff. Denied – by his difference – access to Venice's normal channels of social opposition, he takes refuge in a form of hatred which he converts to a political science. He is sustained by the secret and individual rage and loathing which is possible for any individual who is expelled from or rejected by the social centre.

Part II of this book is an attempt to deal with Shakespeare's construction of a society under siege by its own oppressed classes and individuals. The Cade rebellion of *2 Henry VI*, where the poor rise up in violent rage against those who keep them poor, is the egregious example within the plays of a class war. Political implications of that war are vividly and directly confronted in the play – poor people attempt to take over the government of the country. Their leader is predictably corrupt and wishes to replace the present king with himself as king. In the cases of *King Lear* and *Timon of Athens*, however, the struggle between patrician and plebeian cultures,[4] between cultures of wealth and poverty, takes more complex and subtle forms. As Cade seeks to rise out of poverty through violence, Lear and Timon have poverty thrust violently on them. To Cade, despite his frenzied push for revolution, personal wealth is revealed to be his highest value. Lear comes close to a repudiation of wealth and of the politics that have sustained his wealth and power until now, but he has no weapons to fight against having that wealth and its concomitants restored to him. Timon's repudiation of the ideology of money is venemously absolute. In each case, however, the lives of the protagonists are ultimately subordinated to the overriding authorities of wealth and the power only it can support. Monarchy is restabilized after some negotiation of values and cultural forms: the restoration or recovery of monarchical structures through pressure and threat point to the existence of the struggle against patrician domination. It points also, in the cases of each of these plays, to the continued presence of the conflict that initiated the struggle in the first place. The shoring up of the flagging monarchies of *King Lear* and *Henry VI* supplies evidence of collusion within the upper classes which are protecting themselves against their own poor. Reuniting the nation always means bringing the poor into line. Timon is simply one colossal example of that patrician culture which requires the plebeian world for its own uses and for its own self-definition. The bitter and confused conclusion of his life while interrogating, as it does, the complex functions of wealth and power, provides chiefly the invigorating and scarifying illuminations of pure rage, rather than those of a reasoned politics.

Part III attempts to analyse the phenomenon of deviancy within the political contexts of *Measure for Measure*, *Twelfth Night*, *Othello*, and *The Winter's Tale*. In each case there intrudes into a smoothly functioning political arena some hideous but human sexual monstrosity which threatens to unhinge the mechanism that holds the social formation together. The largeness and flexibility of the society of Vienna is menaced by the sexual abnormality which invades its highest echelon of power. The world of the play is nearly destroyed by sexual desperation at the top, a fact which throws into question the value of the hierarchical structure itself. Othello and Leontes bring into play the deforming passion of sexual jealousy which appears to have become an agent for the maintenance of a patriarchal individualism. The class structure, implicit in both plays with their intensely realized system of individual pos-

sessivism, is held together by the use of women as essential coun-
ters in the structures of wealth and power which sustain the
political culture of class.

Sensuality also nearly destroys Malvolio who understands it as a
means to social advancement. He recognizes the corruptive potential of sexual desire, and he hopes to make use of Olivia's 'desire'
for himself as a way of disturbing the social hierarchy. He provides
an example of the latent function of desire, of how it can be
employed as an agent of social change. Where Angelo, Othello and
Leontes become almost insane with sexual passion, Malvolio calcu-
latingly recognizes sexual passion as a means of overcoming the
social barriers that class and money have placed in his way. It is
interesting that where spontaneous, uncontrollable and violent
sexual desire ultimately produce forgiveness (even in the case of
Othello), when that desire is known and used rather than felt, as in
Malvolio's case, forgiveness is not granted. Sexual desire is as
political as it is psychological; it is imbricated in political codes and
practices partly as a means of asserting male superordinacy within
the system of class opposition. In one sense, Malvolio's crime is
that he feels too little of desire and knows too much.

The opposition of the classes is nevertheless always symbiotic.
Rich and poor, strong and weak, depend upon each other. E. P.
Thompson refers to this mutuality when he writes, 'There is a sense
in which rulers and crowd needed each other, watched each other,
performed theatre and countertheatre to each other's auditorium,
moderated each other's political behaviour'.[5] This active, recipro-
cal relationship is the source of much confusion and conflict in
the plays, and is a constant, if unstated, theme of the following
chapters.

Notes

1. The matter of the origins of Liberalism is referred to in Chapter 8.
2. C. B. Macpherson, *The Life and Times of Liberal Democracy* (Oxford: Oxford University Press, 1976).
3. For me the cry of Political Correctness, a putative left-wing fascism, is a bogus creation of right-wing, chiefly American, academics and journal-ists. They have invented the spectre of an academic world dominated by the left, a situation where hiring, tenure, publication, and academic success are contingent on adherence to left-wing politics. Though there undoubtedly have been left-wing abuses in these areas, these are

so few in number, and so hugely outweighed by abuses by the historically and presently dominant academic fraction, as to be negligible. Minority academics – women, people of colour, and those of the left – remain relatively marginal in academic life notwithstanding the conservative clamour to the contrary.

4. The old terms 'patrician' and 'plebeian' recover useful currency in E. P. Thompson's recent *Customs in Common*. He argues, chiefly in the context of eighteenth-century history, that these terms are more precise and freer of the ideological baggage of the terms currently in vogue like ruling class, working poor, etc. *Customs in Common* (New York: The New Press, 1991), pp. 16–97.

5. Thompson, *Customs in Common*, p. 57.

Part I

2
Othello's Suicide

Soft you, a word or two:
I have done the state some service, and they know't;
No more of that: I pray you in your letters,
When you shall these unlucky deeds relate,
Speak of them as they are; nothing extenuate,
Nor set down aught in malice; then must you speak
Of one that lov'd not wisely, but too well:
Of one not easily jealous, but being wrought,
Perplex'd in the extreme; of one whose hand,
Like the base Indian, threw a pearl away,
Richer than all his tribe: of one whose subdued eyes,
Albeit unused to the melting mood,
Drops tears as fast as the Arabian trees
Their medicinal gum; set you down this,
And say besides that in Aleppo once,
Where a malignant and a turban'd Turk
Beat a Venetian, and traduc'd the state,
I took by the throat the circumcised dog,
And smote him thus.

(V, ii, 339–57)[1]

Othello's suicide engages a knotty complex of social, political and cultural issues. Far from resolving the political and cultural dilemmas of the drama, it exacerbates them and raises more questions than it answers. In that extended moment, his dagger poised to strike himself, Othello drags into the play a memory buried deep in his pre-play past that is of such brutality and hate-filled violence as to link this so-called 'restored' Othello with the crude, tortured brute who struck his wife in Act IV, scene 1 rather than with the noble Roman he exhorts his audience to remember.

The malignant and turbanned Turk exists as a remembered

victim of the Moor. The words, 'smote him thus', bring Othello
into a definitive identification *with* his former victim, murdered for
beating a Venetian and traducing, we presume, the *Venetian* state
in his (the Turk's) own city of Aleppo. Othello, the black Moor,
once murdered a black Turk for 'traducing' the white Venetian
state in the black city of Aleppo. (I use the racial terms black and
white in their current sense, which I take to be little different from
their seventeenth-century sense.) This Turk has a history; he is, in
short, more than merely an enabling figure of the suicide. He
possessed an identity separate and different from Othello. He was
circumcised; he wore a turban; he was violent; he was stronger
than the Venetian he beat and less strong than Othello; he hated
the Venetian state; he was stabbed to death by Othello. As a Moor,
Othello was circumcised, once were a turban, and once, perhaps,
'traduced' the Venetian state before becoming its servant.

In Othello's suicide an intense drama of self-hatred is played
out. Instead of restoring his morally and emotionally battered self,
the suicide is a culmination of the assault made on him by the
contending political and psychological stresses that have been
brought into play. Othello and *Othello* can be seen as the complete
triumph of the white world's ethos of individualism. The black
man/character, separated by nature from the white hegemonic
civilization, is whirled and buffeted by confusion and contradiction. He is loved and feared for his warriorship, but hated and
feared for his colour.

The dichotomies suggested by the black-and-white facts and
images of the play establish a dramatic world and political structure whose vocabulary tends to sustain literality and monologic
interpretation. No one in the play is more susceptible to this mode
of thought than Othello himself. It is and has been a means of
evasion necessary for his survival as a participant in the white
world who has betrayed the people he was brought up with.
Othello is presented as a willing instrument of white domination
and a credulous, enabling tool of white civilization. He is used by
the Venetian state to sustain that domination against its black
enemies. *Othello* uses Othello to support another of the pillars of
white domination, that of the dangers of miscegenation.

The final and total success of white culture is contained in the
single abusive phrase, 'the circumcised dog', which reaffirms a
white construction of the remembered event. No doubt or hesita-
tion informs Othello's recollection. On the contrary, the relish with

which he recovers his own ambiguous blackness through the agency of suicide only serves to reify and intensify the colour divisions of the drama. It is no accident that Othello is referred to as 'the Moor' far more often than as Othello. For whatever the situation, Othello's colour and foreignness are the immediate means of situating him in relation to the play's other characters. He is always different. Martin Orkin, in line with a majority of critics of the play, argues that the racist sentiment in the play is confined to Iago, Roderigo, and Brabantio.[2] This kind of analysis, however, depends entirely upon verbal construction. Simply, the racial sentiments of other characters are not tested. Polite racism, a speciality of Western industrial societies, precisely forbids the verbal expression of racist sentiment during the practice of racial discrimination. The result is an appearance of racial justice without the inconvenience to white domination that this would entail. In South Africa, to use an egregious but pertinent example, the moral justification of apartheid always hinged on the proposition that the races should be kept 'separate but equal'. Equality was desirable because fair; but separateness, on a host of religious, ethnic, political, and psychological grounds, was the essence of the ideology. 'Separate but equal' was recognized by some to be a contradiction in terms, but the managers of apartheid adhered tenaciously to the slogan, creating a polity of separateness that is anything but equal. In *Othello*, it is this same notion that is teased and worried by the white Venetians in their contemplations of the black warrior. The play, as many a critic has noted, is full of the evidence and rhetoric of racial tolerance; evidence of how Othello is *accepted* by the white world. The most famous such evidence is also the phoniest: 'I think this tale would win my daughter too.' (I, 3, 173) This is lip-service of a supersubtle kind which plays into as it acknowledges the existence of a complex racial politics of dominance and submission. Shakespeare has hit upon the pivotal issue of racial relations – miscegenation. Saying, as the duke does, that one's daughter might have been seduced by the gorgeous rhetoric of a married man is no more than a declaration of admiration for his rhetoric – that is, it is perfectly safe to say it.[3] The duke's identification with Brabantio is hollow. And yet the question of the taboo against racial mixing is given a new, sharp focus by this intervention. For the most contradictory and complex social taboo in Western societies is the taboo against interracial marriage. It is especially strong in constructions of fathers contemplating the marriages of their daughters to black men whose sexual potency is an essential part of white racial mythology. The myth is paradoxically designed to repel white women – black men are sexually insatiable and a woman who sleeps with one is feeding her baser, animal passions.[4]

At the outset, it is clear that the state has nothing to fear from Othello while he has much to fear from it. For the demand on Othello for conformity is greater than it is for any other character; the evident penalty for non-conformity is hazard and difficulty as his whole courtship and marriage of Desdemona shows. Othello's acceptance in Venice depends upon him being *extraordinary*. Those critical and theatrical attempts (Jonathan Miller's BBC *Othello* comes to mind) to make Othello almost white, arab rather than negro, dusky rather than brown, are themselves examples of the racism that they sometimes attempt to condemn.[5] Racial difference is a ubiquitous problem. No character does not refer to Othello's racial difference and separateness. Such references, however apparently benign, fulfill one of the chief dogmas of white domination. They always reconstruct difference and separateness; they always put a schism between Othello and the white power structure. Thus even benignity – like the duke's – on racial matters in a situation where Othello poses no threat is automatically self-serving. While Othello conforms to state politics and state racial policy he is allowed to be secure. While he continues, in other words, to regard the world of black, circumcised men as his enemy, he is the darling of the state. When, however, he breaches this politics, he increases his own danger in and to the Venetian state. Venice is stronger in having a black general to fight a black enemy. Just as the fact of the American military being led by a black general in, say, Grenada or Iraq, is by itself a powerful statement about the American state: it ends up sustaining the value of white power in the world while it simultaneously promotes the idea of racial equality. Othello's function is rhetorically similar.

In other words, the most frightening element of Othello's last speech is the perception contained in the realization that he himself is a traitor, both to Desdemona and the white world *and* to the black world in which he grew up. The 'circumcised dog' is both the malignant Turk slain by Othello and Othello himself who traduced the state and the Othello who traduced his black origins by marrying the white woman thus traducing the black world of his birth. With his suicide Othello proclaims the triumph of the white civilization he has traduced. And, indeed, it is the *mimetic* nature of his suicide that supplies the crucial evidence of the defeat and the failure of the Moorish and Turkish cultures in the play. Othello kills himself, as white cultural tradition dictates he ought to do. But in his self-abasement – recovering his own blackness – he offers that white civilization, as on a platter, a powerful vindication of itself.

Why 'circumcised'? Why this emphasis on the penis – someone else's *and* his own if the powerful, authoritative identification is to acquire the perfect symmetry he aspires to – in the last seconds of Othello's life? Part of the answer is, of course, convention: this is a common mode of abuse in the literature of the period in which *Othello* was written. Circumcision was the hidden but material sign of difference between the conflicting black and white, Christian and non-Christian, civilizations. The heathenism of the heathens was engraved on their mutilated bodies as physical and incontrovertible evidence of their savagery and their sexual potency. Plays especially abound with reference to the circumcised pagans of the black world. Also, this index of phallic difference – hidden though it is – marks the gap between the uncircumcised world of white Christian men and the black, Jewish, and heathen worlds of barbarism, cruelty, dishonesty, and sexual vice.

Thus, in the abusive frenzy of his suicide, Othello most becomes the world he has adopted just as he paradoxically proclaims his unworthiness to be a part of it. In the language of hatred which accompanies his suicide, he concentrates a plethora of racially motivated slanders, including the stereotypes by which the black world is distinguished from the white. While the play itself has disturbed these images by its construction of a mysterious and complex black world, the last speech of the hero reasserts them in a characteristically reductive form that tends to dispel the mystery and the difficulty. Killing himself as he killed the malignant and turbanned Turk, in his own mind Othello becomes the loathsome black man of white mythology. The black man reverts to stereotype in this final moment: he is brutal, treacherous, sexual human nature, uncivilized by Christian and Venetian values. The image of the Turk in his own land rising up against the occupying Venetian has none of the saving imagery of resistance to the tyranny of white colonialism which it has acquired in this century. Instead, his violence against the Venetian and the Venetian state is evidence of his barbarism, of how he has deserved his status as a barbarian. The dominant culture triumphs most potently in the idea of the civilized black man destroying his barbaric Other, demonstrating, incidentally, that the civilized black man is a contradiction in terms. For certainly, one of the lessons it is possible to take from the play, and that has been taken from the play, is that the black man cannot be trusted because, however you civilize him, he is still black underneath and will throttle a white woman out of the jealousy to which he is peculiarly susceptible. Certainly, while the play complicates and complexly contradicts the truism, this is the point that Othello makes out of his *own* life through passionate identification with his former victim. This is a crucial element of one powerful aspect of the politics of the play. White civilization vindicates itself through the suicide of the black protagonist. A black man kills a white woman and then kills himself upon the recognition that he is, after all, only a black man. Out of such narratives is much of the literature of race made. The last lines of Othello's suicide speech are a tragic asseveration of his own *racial* inferiority. The speech distills many of the racial issues raised by the more obvious and brutal racists of the play like Iago, Brabantio, and Roderigo. Its impact is wholly contingent upon the blackness of Othello. Because the words are spoken by a black man, they transform the event and the actors in it. The words 'circumcised dog' are, surely, racial abuse, and would be more readily recognized as such were the words uttered by a white man. They, and the other words preceding the stabbing, possess the dangerous potential of satisfying an ideological quest for evidence of hierarchical racial difference. They are words which sustain the ideology of the power structure and warn against disturbing the universe through interference with the racial balance of its structure. Othello *becomes* the Turk, the alien, the circumcised enemy to the state because of his blackness which enables him to close the gap between himself and the turbanned Turk.

The play is obsessively about race, verbally and visually. Love and death are inevitable concomitants of race in this play. No perception, no subject, no assumption can be apprehended in a racially neutral context. The black hero is simply too powerful and disturbing a presence in the text or onstage. The words 'black' and 'Moor' are too culturally loaded in this play – like the word 'Jew' in *The Merchant of Venice* – to be employable in a neutral, non-ideological context. Sexuality, for example, automatically becomes racial when a black participant is present. Conflict and hostility, amity and love are also racial under this condition. Social hierarchy has to be revised and stretched to incorporate the stranger (unless he dwells at the bottom which is always infinitely capacious). This stranger, however, facilitates his own inclusion by his adoption of the manners, habits, and customs of the white tribe. What is radical, what is alarming, is the cost to himself of that adoption. In the steady progression towards his suicide, Othello reveals a vestigial pride in the memory of his former self. That pride, which is most vividly exhibited in the wonderful and shamelessly self-aggrandising senate speech, where Othello makes a virtue of his difference, is slowly eroded and transformed into shame. The brave black man has so completely fallen under the spell of whiteness – embodied in its extreme forms in Desdemona and Iago – that by the end of the play his own blackness is hateful and terrible to him; it is responsible, in part, for his terrible crimes against the white civilization of Venice.

There are two racial mythologies in dialectical contention in the course of the play. The one belongs chiefly to Iago as spokesman for the most flagrant, articulate, and slanderous construction of racial difference. The other, though more grandiose and romantic, is the weaker, more vulnerable narrative of Othello himself,[6] which constructs racial difference along precisely opposite lines to those set down by Iago. The collision of the two arguments brings about the breakdown of Othello, who finally submits to Iago's stronger position, having validated it through *predictable* 'racial' behaviour which he and all others, including the audience, have witnessed. The ending of the play possesses the privileged authority of all endings. It poses as a definitive argumentative conclusion, a synthesis in fact.

This synthesizing tendency of the conclusion is remarkably and powerfully reinforced verbally, visually, and dramatically by the introversion of Othello's suicide and its aural and visual accompaniments. Everything about Othello's last words strains towards a resolution of the dilemmas and contradictions that have erupted in the course of the action. The pursuit of meaning upon which he has been passionately bent seems to terminate in the act of stabbing himself. All his effort seems to concentrate upon this penultimate act of his life as though it were, in fact, his last act. The ritual of public suicide performed to the accompaniment of a diatribe against himself in a frightful inversion of the practice of self-vindication lends the moment an air of finality typically associated with rites that are absolute and definitive. For suicide is, obviously, a resolution, and Othello's posits for a moment the notion that his death will bring a restoration of moral and racial harmony to this world. The 'smote him thus' followed by Lodovico's 'O bloody period!' (358) supplies not merely the illusion of completeness, but also the authoritative and definite statement that resolution or completeness have been achieved. Lodovico, the man who utters the last words and directions of the play comments upon the aggressive and apparently absolute finality of the performance that has just been witnessed. Furthermore, the language of the suicide brings the multiguities of the drama into a single focus, uniting and condensing multiplicity of identity into unity. Othello, becoming his Other, merging his selves into a single loathed self, is eloquent. Even racially there is an apparent resolution to the play's fragmentation and difference as the black race is expunged or extinguished here no less thoroughly than the Turkish enemy in the storm before Cyprus. The suicide provides the momentary illusion that Othello has finally recovered that lost self so vividly depicted, as Stephen Greenblatt notes, in the discourse of his incoherent ravings.[7]

But the suicide is not Othello's last act. As Desdemona seems to die twice, so Othello, having stabbed himself, lives to speak two lines that destabilize the certainties and monologisms of his suicide speech. For in his last two lines Othello dramatically recovers doubt:

> I kiss'd thee ere I kill'd thee, no way but this,
> Killing myself, to die upon a kiss.

> (359–60)

The lines effectively challenge the dense certitude of the suicide speech. Like that speech they draw upon memory and make the attempt to reconcile memory and the past with present experience. 'Kill' and 'kiss', are heard four times in those two lines. They are always powerful words in the language, and are made even more so in such violent conjunctions as this.

The doubt created in these two lines extends backwards into the certainties of the play as a whole. As Othello's previous lines demolish all vestiges of self-worth, these last words interrogate that absoluteness by recovering the fragments of positive value which litter the world of his suicide. In recalling his love of Desdemona at last, Othello is, almost incidentally, also reasserting his own potential value. The joy of the two lines is a recognition of possibility. Othello's lifetime is a search for wholeness, for a single and unshakeable meaning, a faith by which he can live and which he momentarily believes himself to have found in Desdemona. It is thus ironic that in the explosion of certainty expressed in these lines Othello finds relief. While certainty brings its own form of salvation in passionate self-disgust, so an even greater relief lies in the challenge to that emotion. For here Othello recovers a sense of his own value with the recognition that for all his present misery, there once was joy. With this awareness, the whole racial politics of the drama is suddenly renegotiated. The doubt that suffuses the action and thought of the drama on all levels is itself called into question. A clear, simple, single truth uttered by the dying man is brandished like a beacon. The lines function for Othello as a resolution, an indication that the dreadful difficulty of his life has been solved.

Othello's wonderment at the hope that she loved him and his consolation derived from the memory that he kissed her – valued her sufficiently – before he destroyed her, have given comfort to many readers attempting to wrest a meaning from the play. Is it, however, too far-fetched to read the last words of Othello in the same light as we might read the words Lear speaks to Cordelia when he finds her waiting for him after his mad night? Looking at Cordelia, Lear calls her a 'soul in bliss'. His anguish and self-loathing, in other words, are not so extreme as to deprive him of the intimations of heaven. Othello's last words, that is, are a way not so much of redeeming his memory of Desdemona as of recovering his idea of himself. Othello's response to his deed of murder, i.e. his suicide in the Roman style, is an ultimate and futile gesture of obeisance. His suicide is a kind of homage to the patriarchal order. All Venetian men might look at Othello's corpse and say, 'There lies a noble Roman, even though he's black.' The style of Othello's suicide, its motive, declared and speculated, is an affirmation of the politics which lie outside his control, the politics, that is, that have made and controlled him.

A deconstruction of that suicide yields a multiplicity of opposing and contradictory illuminations which are at odds with Othello's absolutist readings of his own action. On a purely specular level, the black general, surrounded by white Venetian men and the corpses of two Venetian women, killing himself in the style dictated by white tradition and uniting himself to it by physically embracing the corpse of the white woman whom he has murdered is a dramatic image which tends to reaffirm white patriarchal values with a vengeance. Othello's suicide and, in it, his return to his white wife with his last tragic words, all point to his passionate insistence on his individual self as the source of the disaster. Iago is to be tortured, presumably to death. Things have been put back into place, the stranger has been eliminated, and justice will prevail.

Othello has deviated from the norms established by these Venetian men, and several people have had to pay the price for his errors. What could be more vivid a demonstration of the resilience of Venetian patriarchy than Lodovico's arbitrary bestowal of Othello's fortune on Gratiano, Desdemona's uncle?

> Gratiano, keep the house,
> And seize upon the fortunes of the Moor,
> For they succeed to you.

> (V, 2, 366–8)

This is an important point. For the whole question of property and how it is defined underlies the play's original conflict, and raising it at this juncture recomplicates what has begun to seem straightforward. The play, at the last, closes in upon itself. The individual as subject, as a complex of ideological formations rather than a single essential self, is momentarily produced to contradict Othello's own simplifications. It is as though the play has outsmarted its hero, as though his quest for justification and meaning – a quest common to heroes – has left him blind to the complexity of the world he has just left. The last lines he speaks indicate that his search for meaning has been successful precisely at the moment that the text renders the idea of the search futile by its production of sweeping and irreconcilable contradictions about human value and life's verities. The consolidation of Othello's property with that of Brabantio's and Desdemona's surviving relative represents a reversion to the material norms that have governed the culture that produced the tragedy. These same norms have supplied codes of heroism by which the materialism is glamourized and sustained. One distinguishing mark of the hero is that he accepts the glamour or the immaterial substance of the codes of materialism as real and independent. The ordinary character is less quick to separate such codes and more easily finds a means to make a compromise between material and heroic codes. Othello is a hero, and his suicide magnificently proves his devotion not just to love and Desdemona, but to love and Desdemona as they are constructed within materialist cultures. Othello's suicide is the killing he wished to commit when he breathed his music over Desdemona's sleeping body: it is a sacrifice to individualism and patriarchy, and it solidly identifies him as a proud son of the culture that produced these values.

There are, however, several things wrong with this picture. It is remarkable, for example, how smoothly events move towards completion, the kind of conclusion in which no strands are left untied, in which a summation, such as Lodovico's, gives the impression of restored cohesion. But it is no accident. The text *appears* to be complicit with the values which Othello proclaims in his dying moments by assigning all authority to so palpable a spokesman for the conservative Venetian polity as Lodovico. The suicide itself, a culturally loaded action and phenomenon, is more than an act of despair and self sacrifice. Suicide is also society's means of recovering social cohesion – that is, contrary to appearance, it is not a pure act of individual will, but hedged with convention, discourse, tradition, and social compulsion. The suicide, especially when he is a murderer whose violence threatens to disturb social balance, becomes a sacrificial victim of the community into whom is concentrated the impulse towards social upheaval. René Girard writes that 'All sacrificial rites are based on two substitutions. The first is provided by generative violence, which substitutes a single victim for all the members of the community. . . . As we know, it is *essential* [my emphasis] that the victim be drawn from outside the community.'[8] Othello's suicide plays conveniently into the hands of the Venetian society and as such it transforms him into the kind of sacrificial victim Girard is describing. It is immediately used (by Lodovico) to affirm the absolute need for social conformity. The family of Brabantio, Desdemona, and Gratiano is, in a sense, restored as a cornerstone of the Venetian society. Their misfortunes are categorized as the consequences of the unadulterated evil of Iago, but their property remains safely in the hands of one of them to be passed on intact. Thus, once again, does individualism serve the polity. The language of Lodovico's last words is replete with images of evil as an uncontainable natural force, represented as residing in Iago. He is a Spartan dog, 'More fell than anguish,

hunger, or the sea' (363), a 'hellish villain' (369). Thus, then, does
the 'Official Version' of the events of the tragedy maintain control
of the instruments of propaganda. According to this version the
tragedy is a result of the conflict engendered by black naivete,
female sexual appetite, and the forces of good and evil. This way of
seeing the tragedy ends up sustaining the patriarchal ideal that
father knows best.

However, as we have seen, there are ways in which the text
subverts the ideologies of individualism, ways in which it challenges the certitudes of patriarchy. The sheer weight of patriarchism as it bears down on woman and stranger is revealed as a kind
of omnipotence. There is no alternative but to accept its laws and
codes, for to defy these is to risk life. In patriarchal terms, the
original sin of this play is Desdemona's flight from her father. This
threatens and weakens the formation and it is this that is dealt with
in the drama. It is, however, also implicit in Desdemona's flight
that the rule of fathers has created the very resistance that necessi-
tates this flight from the father; that an oppressive force applied
from above *creates* its own resistance as it crushes it. Oddly
enough, Othello is most free when he is most dangerous, when he
feels that patriarchy has betrayed him. When he learns, for example, that Venetian women let God see the tricks they dare not show
their husbands, Othello feels the hopeless inadequacy of the ideology he has embraced. But there again, that freedom expresses itself
in terms that ultimately only validate patriarchy further. When
Othello is not behaving like a Venetian, he is a barbarian who beats
his wife and breathes mad destruction and brutality. When Othello
releases himself from the fetters of Venetian civilization, he tumbles into chaos and deformation. The power of patriarchy is nowhere more obvious than in those moments of mad rage. For it is
there that the text indicates the omnipotence of the patriarchal
structure and its inflexibility.

The alternative to the suffering and raging is the comfortable
norms of the structure. The wildness of Othello and, indeed, the
sheer wrongness of Othello, are evidence of its limits. Othello's
transgressions are excursions beyond those limits and end up
validating the practice of conformity that keeps asserting itself. It is
somewhat paradoxical that while the form of patriarchy as obtains
in the Venice of the play values individualism such as Othello's
and, for that matter, Iago's, it also rigidly contains that individual-

ism within a structure of collectivism designed to limit and determine individuality. Othello's suicide, in this context, is the most conformist gesture of the play. It indicates powerfully the limit of individual action, and in doing so it reintegrates Othello into the social nexus. Othello's suicide is utterly predictable because Othello's adherence and devotion to the codes of the Venetians is so deeply felt, so wholehearted, and, because he is a stranger, so severely tried. In killing himself Othello is seeking to recover himself. Sadly and ironically he is doing just the opposite; in embracing white ideals with his suicide Othello is denying his other selves, that complex of codes that has made him what he is.

Notes

1. All Shakespeare quotations are from the Arden editions, published by Methuen and Company.
2. Martin Orkin, 'Othello and the "plain face" of Racism,' *Shakespeare Quarterly*, 38 (1986), pp. 166–88.
3. Karen Newman persuasively argues for the link between black male sexual monstrosity and female desire as an ideological formation of the Venetian patriarchy: 'Othello internalizes alien cultural values, but the otherness which divides him from that culture and links him to the play's other marginality, femininity, remains in visual and verbal allusion.' ' "And wash the Ethiop white": femininity and the monstrous in *Othello*,' *Shakespeare Reproduced: The text in history and ideology*, edited by Jean E. Howard and Marion F. O'Connor (New York: Methuen, 1987) p. 151.
4. English writing reverberates with examples of a female tendency to licentiousness. In, for example, Trollope and Agatha Christie, women are accused of being attracted to the kind of man men have no use for. The man in each case, say Lopez in Trollope's *The Prime Minister* and Costello in Christie's *The Spider's Web*, are dark, foreign, sexually dangerous. In each case, it is declared to be natural that women should be attracted to them. Karen Newman is eloquent on the way in which white culture situates these dark men and white women in opposition to stability.
5. See Newman on Ridley's racism in his introduction to the Arden *Othello*, as well as the connections between racism and seventeenth-century European economy.
6. Joel Fineman explains Othello's vulnerability as a kind of inherent emptiness: 'This evacuating clarification of Othello, most fully realized at this moment when the hero names his name, is what gives Othello his heroic tragic stature, at the same time however, as it specifies the

way in which Othello, as a tragic hero, is inflated with his loss of self.'
'The Sound of "O" in *Othello*: the Real of the Tragedy of Desire',
October, 45 (1988), p. 81.

7. Stephen Greenblatt, *Renaissance Self-Fashioning from More to Shakespeare*
(Chicago: University of Chicago Press, 1980), p. 245.

8. René Girard, *Violence and the Sacred*, translated by Patrick Gregory
(Baltimore: The Johns Hopkins University Press, 1977), p. 269.

3
The Question of Shylock

As a sixteen-year-old schoolboy in Pretoria, I was required to study *The Merchant of Venice*; it was the prescribed Shakespeare text for matriculating students throughout the Transvaal. In a class of thirty boys, I and two others were Jews and, because of this, much of the teaching and discussion of the play was directed at us – not hostilely, but self-consciously, perhaps, as though the class would have been more comfortable if we had not been present. I have noticed, as a teacher myself, the difference it makes to the class when there is a black student present during the teaching of *Othello*. The class is more alert and self-conscious because of the presence of the black student, especially during the inevitable discussions of miscegenation that the play produces. The usually unspoken question to the white students is 'How would your parents react if you were to arrive home with a black boy/ girlfriend?' It creates discomfort and unease for most of the white middle-class Canadians for whom the idea of an interracial romantic relationship is quite foreign.

South African whites are notoriously insensitive on racial issues and, notoriously, they are compelled from an early age into racist modes of thought. In 1958, the previous and present South African Prime Ministers had been openly associated with pro-Nazi activities and sympathies – one, John Balthazar Vorster, had served a jail sentence for his role in supporting the Nazis during the war – but managed to maintain their positions easily, being surrounded by powerful public men with similar alliances. As was the not bad practice of the time, we read our plays aloud in class, parts being taken by different readers. My most vivid memory of that experience was the acute embarrassment I felt at the constant, deafening, repetition of the word *Jew*. Having to read it aloud myself only exacerbated the shame, since it seemed to me that it was almost always used as a term of opprobrium. My father, however, a cultured and well-read man, assured me that there was something defective in my reaction. He venerated Shakespeare, knew long passages by heart, and was convinced that *Merchant* was a play that demonstrated that Shakespeare realized that Jews were like other people. Of course, he trotted out the 'Hath not a Jew eyes' speech, and how could I argue? It seemed conclusive to a sixteen-year-old who had been taught to want to like Shakespeare. And I accepted the party line.

In Jewish cultural circles, Shakespeare was well known, much discussed, and much translated into Yiddish. Jewish writers and critics and their followers dismissed charges of Shakespeare's anti-Semitism as philistine, pointing out, invariably, that although it was true that Jews were moneylenders, they had been forced into this degrading profession by draconian anti-Semitic laws, of which Shakespeare was clearly aware, which excluded them from the more respectable professions and livelihoods. This well-meant argument derived from the then incontrovertible identification of the author's intentions and beliefs with those contained in his works. In those days it *mattered* that Shakespeare, 'the greatest writer of all time', was also a good man. This kind of thinking, however, had the serious failing of deflecting attention from what was a very interesting and important question. Why had the Transvaal Board of Education chosen *The Merchant of Venice* as a required text for grades eleven and twelve students? Indeed, why had it done so quite so frequently? The play was placed in the curriculum almost every other year. Now, while I don't know the names of any of the members of the board it is safe to assume that there was a majority of government supporters on the board, and a minority of supporters of the now defunct United Party, which had almost identical racial policies to those of the government. There may have been one Jew on the board but no more, and obviously in that time and place, no non-whites.

I was not able to erase the memory of discomfort that the word *Jew* produced in me in class. The word *Jew*, as I later discovered, and related words like *Jewess* and *Hebrew*, is used one-hundred-and fourteen times in the play, giving it a concentration in one play matched by few other Shakespearean keywords. *Nature* is used in *King Lear* thirty-four times, *blood* and *bloody* in *Macbeth* thirty-seven. The first time that the word *Jew* is used is in Act I, scene 3. It is in the first stage direction: '*Enter* Bassanio *with* Shylock *the Jew.*' The reason that Shylock is identified not by his profession but by his religion or race is somewhat complex but interesting. Clearly, in the mind of Shakespeare's contemporaries there would have been little distinction between Jew and moneylender as terms. For while it is well known that by far the majority of moneylenders of the middle ages and later were not Jews, the opprobrium reserved for people who made a living out of usury found useful expression in a term that marginalized such people. The medieval and Renaissance churches had condemned usury and hence it was convenient to pretend that it was a labour reserved for outsiders and foreigners. The deception was maintained notwithstanding the common knowledge to the contrary; it provided a convenient target for the charges of godlessness in what was called a Christian society. It would be pointless to refer to this special kind of categorization as anti-Semitic, and I am not engaged here in 'hunt the Jewbaiter'. But it is, perhaps, valuable to recognize that the word Jew, even in an apparently inoffensive context carries a certain charge. It does not admit of a neutral usage. By contrast, the word 'black', though frequently employed offensively in Shakespeare, can have a nonracial or neutral context when it describes the colour of a thing and not a person. *Jew* has no such flexibility. It is always a person, even when it is used as a verb like 'to Jew' or 'to jew', the derivation, so strongly associated with a perception of Jewish culture and history, determines its connotations. As the play amply demonstrates, the word carried a plethora of negative connotations in the age of Shakespeare. This state of affairs has continued since. And by a process of accretion, inevitably the connotations have deepened. It is not possible to think of many favourable connotations of *Jew* in the English language, though *Jewish* has a number of somewhat ambiguously positive ones such as 'Jewish father', which tends to mean over-affectionate and over-indulgent, but basically kind and loving. 'Jewish mother', though it belongs to Jewish folklore, possesses such decidedly negative implications as to outweigh the positive ones it also possesses. Within Jewish religious or patriotic circles, words like *Jew*, *Jewish* or *Jewishly* will be used favourably, but such are hardly in the mainstream of English usage. The word *Jewishly* is used casually and repeatedly in Anthony Burgess's early novel, *The Doctor is Sick*, to stand for slyly, wolfishly, and ingratiatingly, and carries the easy assumption that all of Burgess's readers will recognize and accept the connotations sympathetically; it is never used, as, say, a chauvinistic rabbi might use it, to mean humanely, lovingly, decently.

Modern history has, of course, exacerbated the difficulty. After the Second World War the Jews, whose existence as a people had almost been extinguished, had to come to terms with a world that

had reacted very complexly and ambivalently towards the final
solution of the Nazis. The world's Jewish population had been
depleted, entire communities had been wiped out, millions of Jews
had been killed and, more to my purposes, millions had been
displaced. Deprived of places to live peacefully, many Jews moved
to Israel; they did so in increasing numbers after it became recognized as a state in 1948. This fact created yet another complication
which needed to be faced in dealing with the renewed anxiety
around the question of anti-Semitism. Israel slowly embarked on
policies towards the Palestinians and the surrounding Arab states
which had the effect of alienating leftist thinkers and activists all
over the world. These were and are the very same people who
tended to be sympathetic to the plight of the Jews in Europe during
the war: people to whom the dogmas of anti-Semitism were
anathema found themselves condemning what Jews the world
over call the Jewish state, siding with the enemies of the Israeli
state against the Israelis: or as many Jews insisted, siding with the
enemies of the Jews against the Jews. The distinctions were too
fine on both sides. To many Jews, left-wing politics seemed anti-
Semitic, to many on the left the Jews refused to make the distinction between anti-Semitism and anti-Zionism. To many on both
sides there were no distinctions admissible. One unhappy consequence of the loss of distinguishing colouring on this issue was
the emergence in many circles of power throughout Europe and
America, especially in such enlightened democracies as England
and France, of a new and respectable anti-Semitism. There was, it
might have seemed, a racial truth in Shakespeare's most famous
Jew. For no one will argue that Shylock is not obdurate, defensive,
insular, aggressive, and relentless in revenge. I can remember an
Israeli colonel, after the Yom Kippur war rather grandly quoting
Shylock for the media: 'Thou call'dst me dog before thou hadst a
cause / But since I am a dog, beware my fangs' (III, 3, 6–7). Such
terms as obdurate and aggressive have frequently been applied to
the Israeli governments, especially since the historic elevation of
Menachem Begin.

The fact of Israel has complicated the Jewish position in the eyes
of the world. When Jews were victims only, it was a luxurious and
easy matter to be on their side, to feel sorry for them. The Israeli
presence in the Middle East, however you may regard it, has
changed that perception. No longer victims, the Jews of Israel have
been successful fighters and aggressors in their region. Jews the

world over have gained a kind of confidence as a result and made their presence felt more strongly in other spheres. Possibly unfairly, but in the minds of Jews and gentiles alike, and anti-Semites from both groups, Jews are spoken of and thought of as somewhat aggressive and pushy. These matters have given rise to renewed forms and degrees of anti-Semitism. And that anti-Semitism has had to do with Shakespeare and Shylock.

In the years immediately after the war, before the solid establishment of the state of Israel, there was a considerable sensitivity around the issue of anti-Semitism. Books, films, and plays which represented the suffering of the Jews were unusually popular. Jewish jokes were not so public, and the discussion of the Jewish conspiracy was muted. In Germany especially, anti-Semitic jokes were held to be in the worst of taste; anti-Semitic practice in the West, however, probably underwent few alterations. Israel's rapid rise as a military power, however, its unexpected military success, produced a kind of confidence among anti-Semites. Nobody loves a winner, and a winner is always fair game. Thus a renewed anti-Semitism became possible because, in an odd way, the Jews were stronger than before and could bear the blows. Besides, now they had Israel, a land of their own, and they could therefore be regarded or treated as a nation rather than a race or a homeless people. Menachem Begin's disgusting practice of invoking the holocaust every time Israeli policy was criticized only exacerbated the loathing many felt for Israeli policy in the region. Recent Jewish leadership and, so far as I can tell, all Jewish settlers in the West Bank, luxuriate in the suffering of Jews of the past, using it shamelessly to justify any- and everything done in Israel that meets with criticism. More often than not, the settlers appear to be extremist American or South African Jews whose actual experience of the Holocaust is vicarious, though this has not lessened their ardour in invoking it at the drop of a hat. The defiant 'never again!' slogan, referring to the death camps, sounds a bit forced when it accompanies the bone-breaking, officially sanctioned, military and police activities directed against stone-throwing teenagers.

And even Shylock reflects something of this trend. The debate about Shylock has largely been between the sentimental version of the character given shape by Edmund Kean in the nineteenth century and the Shylock of popular lore who goes back in his origins to Marlowe's Barabas of Malta. The Shylock of Kean is a basically decent man who has been hounded and tormented by a cruel and prejudiced Christian community in Venice and has seized the chance to fight back which has been given him by an almost casual agreement with the merchant, Antonio. He is a victim. The other Shylock, equally powerful in the popular imagination and equally, or more, present in Shakespeare's play, is a vicious monster filled with hatred who seizes the opportunity to murder a good, kind Christian man whose only crime is a too-great fondness for his friend. In the medieval and early Renaissance drama, Jewish characters – moneylenders or financial giants like Barabas – were endowed with exaggerated noses and bright red hair onstage to keep them firmly tied to the ancient folk traditions which depicted Judas in this way and, of course, to remove any doubt as to their racial difference from the audiences for whom they were presented.

The characterization of Shylock has been at the centre of the debate about whether the play is anti-Semitic. And the debate is fairly well known. Most of it centres on the ambiguity of certain well-known speeches and passages in the play. There are perhaps two speeches which stand at the centre of the controversy. The best known is, of course, the 'Hath not a Jew eyes' speech which is read in the critical and popular literature about the play as either a defense of the sheer, ordinary humanity of the Jews or else as a cruel justification of revenge. The first reading is well known; less well known is the reading which takes the speech to begin not with that famous phrase but with its literal beginning when Shylock is asked by Salario, 'What's [his flesh] good for?' Shylock's response is not always remembered. He replies:

> To bait fish withal, – if it will feed nothing else, it will feed my
> revenge; he hath disgrac'd me, and hind'red me half a million,
> laughed at my losses, mock'd at my gains, scorned my nation,
> thwarted my bargains, cooled my friends, heated mine enemies, –
> and what's his reason? I am a Jew. Hath not a Jew eyes?
>
> (III, 1, 53–9)

Perhaps it is worthwhile to recall the play's constant equation of *Jew* with moneylender, as in that first usage of the word *Jew* in the early stage direction discussed above. The speech, in other words, may convincingly be read and, perhaps, better understood, by the substitution of Moneylender for Jew: 'Hath not a Moneylender eyes?' Well, yes, we may reply, but he also has more money and power than anyone in town, so why should we feel pity for him? Having catalogued the various ways in which Jews are like Christians, Shylock's speech comes to a crashing finale with these last lines:

> If a Jew wrong a Christian, what is his humility? revenge! If a Christian wrong a Jew, what should his sufferance be by Christian example? – why revenge! The villainy you teach me I will execute, and it shall go hard but I will better the instruction.
>
> (III, 1, 62–66)

Shylock's justification of revenge, by the way, is based upon a number of demonstrable lies and false predictions. But above all, we ought to note, it is based upon a clearly stated equation of revenge with villainy. Though there is no indication that Antonio is his friend, or is even polite to him, Antonio's motives for hating Shylock should strike a chord of sympathy in the hearts of anyone who has ever taken out a mortgage – and there is no one, Jew or Christian, who would rather take a mortgage from Shylock than Antonio. Antonio despises Shylock because he lends money out for interest; he exploits people's vulnerability. He makes them indebted to him and then takes advantage of their indebtedness. He is significantly unsurprised that Shylock wants to negotiate merrily around a pound of his flesh, because it is the kind of behaviour he and Venice have learned to expect from the bloodsucking usurer. Indeed, Shylock himself, for all the eloquence of the line, 'and what's his reason? I am a Jew', is missing the boat by a mile unless he understands – as modern audiences, naturally, do not – that Jew *means* gouging moneylender. For he has earlier, in an aside, given his own reasons for hating Antonio, speaking volumes about himself and what the play constructs as his 'Jewish' values:

> I hate him for he is a Christian:
> But *more* [my emphasis] for that in low simplicity
> He lends out money gratis, and brings down
> The rate of usance here with us in Venice.
>
> (I, 3, 37–40)

This speech tends to give a certain substance to Antonio's own assertion that his loathing for Shylock is not primarily racial, but moral (there can be little doubt that until the twentieth century the Jews were regarded by the rest of the world as a different race like, say, the Hottentots). The *us* of that last line refer to the Jews *as* usurers almost by definition.

It might also be noted that the whole emphasis of Shylock's speech is simply wrong, an actual error. He claims that 'If a Jew wrong a Christian, what is his humility? revenge.' The play takes much of its motive energy from a story in which a Jew wrongs a Christian. Shylock strikes an illegal bargain with a Christian merchant who doesn't like him, and he spends much of the rest of his onstage career trying to kill him. He seems to get close. In the court of law where he gets his come-uppance, he sharpens his knife on the sole of his shoe as he slaveringly contemplates the moment when he will shove the knife into the heart of his enemy. (To see Antony Sher, the South African, Jewish, English actor perform this ceremony at Stratford-Upon-Avon was to watch Shylock transform this act of unholy revenge into a sacred Jewish ritual. It intensified the anti-Jewish quality of the play.)

But then what happens is almost the reverse of what Shylock has declared to be an absolute and incontrovertible truth. When Shylock loses the upper hand, and Antonio has the opportunity to return the compliment, Shylock's declaration that when a Jew wrongs a Christian the Christian's response must and will be to take revenge is proven false. Antonio is offered revenge: Portia asks him, 'What mercy can you render him, Antonio?' The first answer comes from the compulsive interjector, Gratiano, who speaks the ancient creed of *lex talionis*, by which Shylock also lives: 'A halter gratis. Nothing else for Godsake!' The halter is the gallows, and the emphatic invocation of God is a sure indication that there is an alternative to mercy. But, in his way, Antonio is merciful: he offers, in rather righteous and hieratic fashion to be sure, clemency to the would-be murderer when he could be offering him death. True enough, the mercy he gives is so hedged with draconian conditions as to amount to a kind of living death, especially the stipulation that Shylock become a Christian. But while many a modern Jewish and non-Jewish critic has regarded this forced conversion as a death sentence, Shylock himself does not see it in this way. (An awful attempt to sentimentalize this moment was offered in Lawrence Olivier's 1972 TV Shylock. When Shylock leaves the stage the audience is given the treat of a rather hysterical Kaddish from the wings to indicate that Shylock is facing his death.)

Antonio's words seem more than anything to emasculate Shylock, they rob him of his energy. But they also rob him of his villainy. In no play of Shakespeare's is a character more humiliated by the author, so stripped of his dignity, than Shylock in the *Merchant of Venice*. Shylock's pathetic response to the mercy offered him by his enemy, Antonio, is dreadful to behold. It is a cruel moment in the drama. Shylock has lived entirely by rage and hatred. His strength has come entirely from the contempt and loathing he has for these Christians. He dominates the stage utterly and completely every time he appears. He is a personification of power and furious intelligence. And yet, when he is offered his life as a gift of mercy from the enemy whom he would have killed minutes before, when he is offered clemency from these despised and weak Christians, he suddenly, unexpectedly, meekly and brokenly accepts it. And it is a dramatic outrage committed on the audience. The author has broken faith with his audience and his character. We read a text with a certain trust in the author. We insist on the bargain being kept. We do not wish to be toyed with and made fools of by the writers whose books we read. But Shakespeare here deforms his character for, I suppose, the convenience of keeping the comedy from drowning in tragic violence. He distorts the direction of the flow. Shylock has a destiny in the play; he is the scourge of righteousness, especially Christian righteousness. This destiny gives him a massive, if terrible, dignity. He is supremely Shylock, the Jew of Venice, and all that that entails. Like a raven he croaks and watches in the court scene as his victim gets closer and closer to his talons. He sharpens his knife on his bootsole. He raises it, ready to plunge it into Antonio's bosom. And then suddenly he is stopped – to the relief, presumably, of all right-thinking people. (Richard Mansfield's Shylock [New York, 1893] dramatically and violently recognized this discontinuity in the play by giving himself a death wound, not present in the text, before leaving the stage.) Portia and Gratiano torture Shylock with his guilt until, when he can stand it no more, he utters his fateful and helpless last speech:

I pray you give me leave to go from hence,
I am not well, – send the deed after me,
And I will sign it.

(IV, 1, 390–2)

This is his worst moment. He is burnt out, craven, beyond hope.
He dwindles into bones before our eyes. The towering Jewish
monster is really just a ludicrous and absurd little Yiddle fearfully
accepting life at any cost. His threats and curses amounted to
nothing but this pathetic little man doddering off the stage, exposed, ashamed, humiliated. And not even Lawrence Olivier sing-
ing Kaddish can give him back his dignity. The audience has been
taught or warned to fear this man who will kill and kill out of
hatred and revenge; now it is told there really was nothing to
worry about in the first place. The audience too has been made to
look a little foolish in its willingness to fear this little pitiable man.
It is all over. And it is all there in the text, in those excruciating and
thin last words that he speaks.

The Shylock we have been following in the play was born or
created for just this moment – to raise his knife and thrust Antonio
in the heart even as his villainy is exposed with, perhaps, a
second's thought. He and we have been primed for a *killing* by
every word he has spoken and that has been spoken about him in
the play. There has to be logical and sequential direction to such
rage and hatred as he has expressed during the drama. This shocking twist is an unnatural and outrageous jolt of our sensibilities and
his own destiny. It transforms the blood-thirsty, flesh-tearing
carnivore into a meek little Jewish man whose existence up to this
point, so movingly and compellingly definite, has been a lie. It
reforms the conception of the Jew that the play has so powerfully
produced. We might consider, by way of contrast, the last moments of Marlowe's Barabas. He goes tumbling magnificently into
the boiling cauldron shrieking defiance: 'Tongue, curse thy fill and
die!" What the *Merchant* leaves us with is an inversion of the notion
of the Jew upon which the entire burden of the play has lain, thus
incorporating the contradictory images of the Jew so viciously
propagated by Julius Streicher: on the one hand the Jew is a
powerhouse of evil and corruption, villainously plotting the subjugation of the Christian world, and on the other he is merely
vermin to be crushed with heel of a Christian/Nazi jackboot.

This is an important point. Because there is, as is well known, disagreement about what the idea of the Jew really is in this play. I cite one example, almost entirely unnoticed in the literature on the drama, of how Shakespeare has given a vivid idea of what 'Jew' means, without precisely drawing attention to it. This fact is exactly what makes the example so pernicious and difficult to deal with. It comes at the end of Act III, scene 1, some sixty lines after the 'Hath not a Jew' speech. Shylock has listened with some relish to a recital of Antonio's financial problems. Tubal, 'another of the tribe' enters and the Christians, Salanio and Salerio, exeunt. Shylock and Tubal talk of Antonio's misfortunes and Shylock's own, which include the fact that his daughter – not much beloved, in my view, but a daughter nonetheless – has run away with a Christian and stolen a large part of her father's fortune. Shylock, unlovelily expresses to Tubal the wish that his daughter 'were dead at my foot, and the jewels in her ear: would she were hears'd at my foot and the ducats in her coffin.' (80–2) The news gets worse and worse for him, but it also gets worse and worse for Antonio whose fortunes, Tubal tells him, 'are certainly undone' (114). In Tubal's recitations of Antonio's misfortunes, Shylock seems to find relief at the prospect of torturing and killing Antonio as some kind of compensation for the wrong done him by his daughter. Indeed, he calls Antonio's disasters, 'good news, good news: ha ha!' (95) Then, finally, as the scene ends, Shylock addresses Tubal as follows:

> go Tubal, fee me an officer, bespeak him a fortnight before, – I will have the heart of him if he forfeit, for were he out of Venice I can make what merchandise I will: go Tubal, and meet me at our synagogue, – go good Tubal, – at our synagogue Tubal.
>
> (115–18)

There are several points to be made here. Shylock gives his motives for wishing to kill ('have the heart of') Antonio, and they reiterate what he has said before. With Antonio out of the way he 'can make what merchandise [he] will', plain and simple. The last sentence uses the word 'synagogue' twice. Let us examine the context of that usage. To most of us, a synagogue is a place where Jews pray, but here the word is rather more than usually charged with meaning. Shylock has been hugging himself with glee – or merely consoling himself – that he can now kill the Christian man who, as

he has told us, 'lends out money gratis'; the man who has bor-
rowed money to help a friend in love achieve the woman he wishes
to marry, who is loved by everyone in Venice except Shylock and –
logically – Tubal; a man who is decent and kind and sweet-
natured, who is, in short, the precise opposite of Shylock himself.
And now, having declared his pleasure at the prospect of killing
this man, Shylock arranges to meet Tubal at the synagogue, where
they both pray, to confirm the arrangements for the legal killing of
this, at least relatively, innocent man.

The exhortation to meet at the synagogue, then, lends a certain
colouration to the meaning of 'synagogue'. It is clearly more than
simply a place of worship. It is the place – in this context – where
unholy, diabolical arrangements take place among *Jewish* mur-
derers. Furthermore, since a play is as much heard as read, there
must surely be some significance attached to the first syllable of
'synagogue', a significance that might explain why it is repeated in
two lines. That last phrase, 'at our synagogue Tubal' is wholly
unnecessary from any point of view except as way of suggesting
that there is some more meaning to the idea of a synagogue than
simply as a place where Jewish people pray to their God. I hope it
is not paranoic of me to say that I hear in the repetition some
deliberate and sinister references to the fabled, but deeply entrenched, Jewish blood rituals that have informed the Christian
imagination since at least the Middle Ages. Thus do religious
worship and bloodletting come into a very powerful, and very
anti-Semitic conjunction and, precisely because the moment is so
ambiguous, there is no critical ingenuity that can undo the implications of such lucid but unstated purposes. No mention of Jews
here, just an apparently casual appointment to meet at the synagogue, which is, it would seem, not casual at all.

The Merchant of Venice has been a bellwether of public sentiment
about the Jews. It is no coincidence that Kean's portrayal of a
sympathetic Shylock should have been popular at a time when a
largely romantic sympathy for the downtrodden should have been
popular – rather perhaps like Dickens's rather sentimental, if well-
meant, sympathy for the poor. It is perhaps interesting and significant that Anthony Sher's Shylock should have coincided with a
notable decline in sympathy for the fortunes of the Jewish state in
the modern world and a concomitant rise in anti-Semitism in the
West. This has taken the form of vandalizations of Jewish public
places like cemeteries, museums, and synagogues, freer public

expression of anti-Semitic sentiment than had been the case since the war, and a rise in understandable and hard-won sympathy for the Palestinians which led all too predictably to the equation of the Jewish people everywhere with the State of Israel and the supporters and citizens of the State of Israel with an increasingly hard-line, right-wing and occupationist Israeli government.

In Kitchener, Ontario, in 1986 a furor arose when, after years of trying, Jewish parents managed to get *The Merchant of Venice* removed from the Junior High School curriculum. They and their small number of non-Jewish allies were successful in having the matter referred to the Provincial Board of Education which has still not come up with a decision about the reasons why or why not this particular Shakespeare play should be *required* reading in the charged context of the classroom. Some Jewish children had been pelted with coins in the schoolyard, and there had been further incidents of this kind at a number of school performances of the play at nearby Stratford, the home of what is arguably North America's major Shakespeare festival. Students reported that the play had taught them a new anti-Jewish vocabulary; for many it confirmed attitudes that had been learned in their homes and on the streets. It was not lost on the rest of the community that Kitchener was heavily populated with the descendants of German immigrants to Canada, and that before the First World War the town with the now impeccably English name had been known as Berlin. These facts lent a slight suggestion of the death camps to the entire incident, which it would not have done without the German presence in the town, and in light of the fact that the drama about the drama had been played out many times in school systems that had no German 'taint'. The year before the fuss about the teaching of the play, John Neville played Shylock in an interpretation that deeply offended many Jewish spectators, and had the *Canadian Jewish News* (the right-wing Jewish affairs gazette that claims to speak for all Canadian Jews) expressing its indignation quite volubly. People were upset. It would seem that such interpretations of Shylock as could disturb Jewish communities and which would not have been countenanced during or immediately after the war in English-speaking communities had become possible once more.

Of course, as anti-Semitism has become somewhat more public in recent years, and as productions of the play which acknowledge its anti-Jewishness have become more acceptable, so too the Jews have changed since the war and since the founding of Israel. The war was fifty years ago and sensitivities have become somewhat hardened on both sides. Like Shakespeare, the Holocaust has become an industry on its own. Books, magazines, entertainment of all kinds, tourism, manufacturing, education have all been affected by the fact of this terrible event. This ought not to be a cause for sorrow. It was an inevitable consequence of the same consumerism which has affected Shakespeare studies and which determines so much about the world we live in. Certainly there has been a good deal of vulgarization of the subject, banal and stupid movies and TV specials, cheap and easy horror in literature or on the screens. In concert with the cheapening there has been the serious and conscientious examination of the event and its causes and effects: there have been the art and literature which have enriched us all, and the historical and philosophical studies. But it is certainly passing into history before our eyes. The survivors are diminishing in number, Simon Wiesenthal has lost his robustness, and, significantly, there is a multiplicity of Chairs in Holocaust Studies in universities all over the world. This last seems to be the most convincing evidence of the present losing touch with the past, this founding of university chairs, worthy though that is, in order to keep alive something that is fading from memory. The town of Kitchener, Ontario will be holding a referendum in the next few months on the question of whether to change its name back to the original Berlin.

Indeed, after the war, though the minds and memories of Europeans and Americans were shot through with images of the death camps and the starved beaten corpses of the victims of the Nazis, no one had ever heard of the Holocaust. There is a good and reasonable case for dropping the word in its Second World War context from the language. A holocaust is a burnt offering, a holy sacrifice. To describe the murder of the six million Jewish victims of Hitler as a holocaust is to endow the event with a quasi-religious, mystical property that empties it of its dirty political reality, a reality which must be faced if it is to be properly understood. It comes, in such circumstances, to belong to mythology and not reality; as such it loses its place in the rational and the real and occupies some kind of transcendent space which romanticizes it and removes it from the realm of normal comprehensible discourse, inviting the pointless speculation that it was the will of God, rather than a palpable, historical, and all too human occurrence.

It may have become possible once again for anti-Semitism *not* to be linked with the death camps. To dislike or hate a Jew because he is a Jew is not necessarily to wish him burnt or gassed or horribly killed. The Boeskys and the Millikens and the Maxwells are crass phenomena of our own time; unlike those literary characters discussed above they are self-created. The great unwritten thing about these odious, noisome crooks is that they are all Jews: but no-one isn't thinking it. Their antecedents in literature are, of course, the Barabases and, most wonderfully, Augustus Melmotte of Trollope's *The Way We Live Now*, who is not only a Maxwell in scruples and moral degeneracy, but who in size, appearance, and gross bullying behaviour is uncannily like the Maxwell we are now reading about in the daily papers, and who kills himself rather grandly and opulently at the end of the novel.

But towering over all these Jewish giants of wickedness and giants of Jewish wickedness is the lonely figure of Shylock. Jews, gentiles, critics, readers, producers, actors, and schoolteachers have always taken from him what they have wanted and, in all probability, they always will do so. His words will continue to be used, as they have been, to demonstrate the sheer humanity of the Jews: they will also be used, as they have been, to demonstrate Shakespeare's prescient awareness of the twisted Jewish psyche.

4

Caliban's Body

That Caliban is physically repulsive is a given of the play. Everyone who comes into contact with him is repelled by his bodily form and shape. Even Ariel, who is stranger, or more inhuman, than Caliban in his ability to fly and hide and change his shape, and is regarded as quaint and delicate, takes it on himself to side with Prospero in oppressing the 'monster' when he and it share a similar fate under the magician's heavy hand. Most complex, perhaps, of all, is Miranda's sense of revulsion against Caliban. Having no memory of men or sense of social behaviour other than those learned from contact with her austere and tyrannical father, it is not clear where her feelings of antipathy for Caliban stem from. Whether he attempted to rape or seduce her – 'violate / The honour of my child' (I, 2, 349–50) – is not reliably reported; our source for this tale is that most biased of all sexual narrators, the young woman's own father. She can recall a pristine time when she coddled and nurtured him, taught him to speak English. With an indignation only matched in the play by that of her father, Miranda reminds Caliban:

> Abhorred slave,
> Which any print of goodness wilt not take,
> Being capable of all ill! I pitied thee,
> Took pains to make thee speak, taught thee each hour
> One thing or other. When thou didst not, savage,
> Know thine own meaning, but would gabble like
> A thing most brutish, I endow'd thy purposes
> With words that made them known. But thy vile race,
> Though thou didst learn, had that in't which good natures
> Could not abide to be with; therefore wast thou
> Deservedly confin'd into this rock,
> Who hadst deserv'd more than a prison.

(I, 2, 353–64)

Among the many striking sources of hostility in this tirade, what seems to stand out is Caliban's failure of gratitude. This is a vicious, furious, and abusive speech addressed to a slave or servant.[1] Miranda pitied this man, who appears to have mistaken pity for affection, as she herself seems to have done. His return was sexual affection – whether violent or not is somewhat ambiguous in the context of hatred and hostility in which this discourse is here placed – which transcended the limits of the understanding of the relationship between Miranda and himself and which, clearly, failed of its purpose. Prospero's statement, 'thou didst seek to violate / The honour of my child', begs many questions. To 'violate the honour' can mean corrupt, seduce, tamper with, have sex with, ingratiate yourself into the sexual favours of, and it can certainly mean force or rape; the latter is the usual interpretation of Prospero's words. Miranda has *learned* from her father to translate Caliban's attempt upon her virtue in terms that agree with her father's. She has been taught to understand this attempt on her virtue as 'racially' determined behaviour.

Although the reason for Caliban's slavery and imprisonment is clear to Prospero, to Miranda Caliban has only committed that crime 'which good natures / Could not abide to be with.' Given the limits of her experience of good natures and her inevitable dependence upon her father for direction on this rather important point in the process of her socialization, we can really never be sure of what precisely Caliban's crime against Miranda was. It would seem that his physical ugliness looms large as an active wrong against Prospero and Miranda, his presumption in aspiring to pollute their European purity is ultimately unforgiveable. Indeed, when a handsome white man presents himself as a sexual object to Miranda she is less than slow in making sexual advances to him, and her father is less than displeased.

It is unsurprising that the hatred of Prospero and Miranda for Caliban should have a sexual source. The romantic interest of the drama represents quite straightforwardly that Prospero is determined to keep his race pure, to marry his daughter to a white European man with the correct social pedigree. Caliban is an actual and potential threat to this ambition. If Miranda should love him, Caliban threatens death to the Prospero line. If Caliban should beget a child off her, the same result follows. Hayden White notes that 'species corruption' has been universally regarded as a degradation of God's plan. 'Since the Creation God fashioned the world and placed in it the various species, each perfect of its kind, the ideal natural order would therefore be characterized by a perfect species purity. Natural disorder, by contrast, has its extreme form in species corruption, the mixing of kinds . . . the joining together of what God in his wisdom had decreed should remain asunder.'[2] There is a widely practised taboo on the mixing of kinds. Thus, to use one extreme but, in the context, relevant example supplied by White, 'men who had copulated with animals had to be exiled from the community, just as animals of different kinds which had been sexually joined had to be slaughtered.'[3] The analogy in human terms is all too familiar in the modern world. Racial, national, and religious mixing have been prohibited for centuries on the grounds of unnaturalness. The modern world finds the concept of unnaturalness somewhat embarrassing and replaces the argument with the more rational but no less persistent and prohibitive arguments taken from sociology and psychology. Racial antipathies, that is, are dressed up in academic robes.

The enforcement of the prohibition is contingent upon the success or failure of the doctrine of the natural. If the subject can be convinced of the validity of the definition of what is natural behaviour and desire, then the possibility of retaining racial purity is strengthened. As the conviction of the subject is weakened, the social consequences become more serious and the purity of the dominant culture or enforcing agencies – government, church, family – becomes endangered. Prospero has essentially indoctrinated Miranda with ideas about the meaning of Caliban's difference from herself and himself. It is a difference that clearly transcends sex. He is a racial, or 'natural' inferior to them both in terms of impulses, desires, and all other natural or biologically determined proclivities. This difference is heightened by his corporeal unlikeness to them.

The known facts about Caliban's body are few but very revealing. He is freckled, he smells like a fish, he is ugly by the European – or human – standards of those who see him, he is 'misshapen' (V, 1, 271), a 'beast' (IV, 1,140); there is a piscine quality about him – both Trinculo and later Antonio regard him as something that has come from the sea. Caliban, according to Prospero, is 'not honour'd with / A human shape' (I, 2, 285–6); that is, there is something monstrous in him. He himself refers to his 'long nails' (II, 2, 166) which he uses for digging. His freckles are the most evident visible mark of his difference though they could be tiny spots of pigmentation or large piebald blots or both. The other physical qualities of Caliban are mainly reported in the form of reactions to him – his smell and look are 'ugly' and repulsive to the Europeans. Curiously enough, for all his bloodthirstiness, he appears to be a vegetarian, eating roots and berries.

Caliban's antecedents in Shakespeare are the creatures of Othello's history – not so much Othello himself – the Anthropophagi and men 'whose heads / Do grow beneath their shoulders', (*Othello*: I, 3, 145–6) wild creatures who are much celebrated and frequently depicted in medieval iconography. He is, in short, a man, much like those men with heads placed in their chests. But he belongs to a different species of men than the Europeans and black men of the plays. His species difference consists in birth markings that loudly and grotesquely identify him as only marginally a man. His most human quality appears to be his ability to learn 'language' or, at least the English language. Reconciling these always fascinating aberrations of humankind with the workings of a wise but unfathomable God was one task assumed by medieval writers. According to Richard Bernheimer, they projected wildness through images of desire released from the trammels of convention but capable, nevertheless, of containing both the benign and the evil properties of wildness simultaneously.[4] To the radical moderns like Marx, Freud, and Nietzsche, Hayden White argues, history was a struggle to liberate men from the oppression of a society originally created as a way of liberating man from nature. 'It was the oppressed, exploited, alienated, or repressed part of humanity that kept reappearing in the imagination of Western Man – as the Wild Man, as the monster, as the devil – to haunt him thereafter.'[5] Sexuality, desire, lust, violence, and, perhaps anomalously, freedom, are both part of Caliban's own conception or reading of himself and very much a part of what is read into him both as himself and as that self as a representative product of his wildness by those who create (teach) him, and those who observe him. The difficulty is to clarify the degree and extent to which his self-conception and self-knowledge are spontaneous, innocent, and 'true' or accurate perceptions of himself and that to which even they are a conception learned from his oppressors, Prospero and Miranda.

Caliban's famous flesh-tearing snarl – 'You taught me language, and my profit on't / Is, I know how to curse. The red plague rid you/ For learning me your language!' (I, 2, 365–7) – constructs more difficulties than it is credited with answering. He inculpates Prospero and Miranda for teaching him language itself *and* for teaching him *their* language. Which is it? His previous oral noise (speech?) is described by Miranda as 'gabble . . . most brutish' (358–9). We do not know if he could curse in his brutish gabble or, for that matter, whether he had occasion for cursing before his subjugation by the European intruders on his island. We are never instructed in this point or in the question of whether Caliban is so much convinced of the superiority of his oppressors that he accepts their description of the sounds he made before he learned their language. If he gabbled, of course, we must assume that he was at least trying to speak, that he was using his organs of speech for the purpose of communicating, however incomprehensibly, with these effete Europeans.

Caliban possesses a memory. It is, in addition, more than just an instinctual memory or reflex; rather it is a capacity to recollect and feelingly to recuperate experiences from the past. Caliban's memory is a fascinating mixture of love and hate, good and bad, sweetness and bitterness. He retains admirably the ability to keep these matters precisely discrete. He recalls initially how he was loved by Prospero, how he was stroked and fed and made much of. And, no less importantly, how he loved Prospero in return, and how, in his love he gave Prospero access to the sweet secret places of his island. He remembers too his mother and the name of her God, Setebos. But, of course, more immediately he remembers the daily cruelty of his oppression. He can be jolted into obedience by the memory of his most recent punishments which take the form of physical pain of different kinds.

Caliban remembers and understands an essential concept of government. He understands what it is to be mastered, to be a servant and slave, and he rebelliously entertains sad fantasies of liberty – under a new master. He believes it is natural that there be servants and masters, and he believes that he is a servant. Thus, when Trinculo and Stephano appear masterful but benign, he simply wishes to change them with Prospero. Prospero's efficacious use of violence to subdue him has done its work. Caliban's nature has been enslaved by fear of physical pain. While there are Europeans with their magic tricks around him, his lot is, by definition, one of servitude. The definition of his place comes from those who possess the power to define and construct authority and culture – Prospero and Miranda.

Thomas Harriot's now famous account of the 'invisible bullets' – probably they were simple colds – which decimated the Algonkian Indians in the sixteenth century, and which helped to place them entirely under the sway of the marauding Europeans, has implications in a consideration of the plight of Caliban.[6] European magic has two forms in *The Tempest*. There is the supernatural magic of Prospero which can control nature and reorder it. And there is the more primitive magic of Stephano and Trinculo which comes in a bottle and can produce euphoria and delusions. The cold virus which can kill Indians and the sack which can drive Caliban into megalomaniacal frenzies demonstrate the strength of the Europeans and the relative weakness of the natives of far-away places. They have the effect, for all the moral disapproval with which they may be viewed, of confirming prejudices about the superiority of white civilization. Caliban's susceptibility to drink and his consequent rages against Prospero are represented in the play as 'racial' proclivities: if he is made drunk his true or 'natural' propensity for violence comes out. This syndrome, all too familiar in the histories of oppression of native peoples all over the world, forms part of a massive body of discourses justifying racial subjugation.

The tension of this play lies precisely in the irreconcilables of the logical and moral opposition upon which the drama of Caliban's desire for freedom rests. Prospero's tyrany is represented as necessary and is justified on the grounds of Caliban's ugliness, potential violence, and species-difference. Yet Prospero's tyranny is harsh and cruel, and, with his capacity for cursing, Caliban has not lost his capacity for suffering. Prospero's presumption in occupying Caliban's island is not ignored or smoothed over, and Caliban's desire to recover his place seems just. But revulsion for Caliban's physicality is universal. The Europeans all regard him as a freak or curiosity, as a member of another species than their own. The consensus of the Europeans as to the repulsiveness of the monster is a powerful vindication of the way he is regarded as inferior. His primitivity is an evidence of the inferiority of his species. He is driven by low, sexual impulses which find expression in a tendency towards simple and palpably stupid solutions to difficult questions, such as his apparently odd, incongruous, and comic notion of freedom as a new master. But behind such ideological matters as liberty and government lies the basic reality of his revolting presence.

Caliban, with his dark ugly body and his unpleasant odours,

forcefully reminds us of the Yahoos of *Gulliver's Travels*. He is a kind of corporealized excrement. His 'freckles' are reminiscent of stains of excrement that linger on his body; his closeness to nature makes him one with the dirt around him. It seems to me at least feasible to argue, *pace* Norman O. Brown, that where human beings are possessions of other men, they fulfill the function of repressed anality. Their (usual) difference in colour and type make them convenient, if unconscious, symbols of and substitutes for the anal product which remains through life an unconscious erotic object. According to Brown, the use by the child in its anal stage of feces as gift, property, or weapon, originates in the anal stage of infantile sexuality and never loses its connection with it. The infant uses feces as property to assert and demonstrate its independence, in the same way that feces as gift can be used to obtain love from another.[7] Caliban supplies this role as symbolic feces to Prospero. 'Thus some of the most important categories of social behaviour (play, gift, property, weapon) originate in the anal stage of infantile sexuality and – what is more important – never lose their connection with it. When infantile sexuality comes to its catastrophic end, non-bodily cultural objects inherit the symbolism originally attached to the anal product, but only as second-best substitutes for the original (sublimations). Sublimations are thus symbols of symbols. The category of property is not simply transferred from feces to money; on the contrary, money is feces, because the anal erotism continues in the unconscious. The anal erotism has not been renounced or abandoned but repressed.'[8]

Property in the form of human beings, especially such human beings as have been constructed as deformed and discoloured, elicits in the owner such ambiguous, repressed erotism as indicated in the phase of infantile anal erotism. The repression finds expression in property like money, or, equally clearly, in the subject human being who is endued by the repressed owner or subjugator with characteristics of the repressed erotic object – the excrement. While hatred and contempt for brown people has surely to do with the fact of the physical difference of subjugated people who are almost always brown, and who almost always possess features that are racially different from and other than those of the white oppressor. That is to say, the slave – and Caliban is a slave – fulfills a suppressed erotic need in the owner by being easily transformable into an object of repressed anal erotism. A slave's body serves the ambiguous purpose of being socially constructable as ugly – the slave–owner defines his own and his slave's culture, decides what is ugly and what is evil – though less overtly it is also simultaneously desirable and sexual. Artistic depictions of slaves and savages by white writers and painters almost invariably construct primitivity and brutality as infused with sexual vitality. It can, I think, be argued that slavery and servitude are primarily designed to separate the cerebral from the excretory functions. The learned loathing for the anal product as we leave infancy makes such separation desirable – indeed we call it normal. The slave and the servant's function, as often as not, is to do the dirty work, clean up the mess, of the master or mistress. Servitude, in this sense, is modernized slavery. People poorer than oneself are paid, rather than compelled, to help maintain the distance between the cerebral and anal selves. Maintaining that distance is one of the chief criteria of civilized behaviour. Hence it is self-serving but common to construct the slave, the Calibans, as belonging to that excremental world almost naturally – i.e. physically and morally.

The sexual vitality of the slave is not so much an inconsistency as an index of ambiguity in the master's relationship with the slave. It is merely one of the ways that the body of the slave fulfills a need which is created by the ownership. In other ways it is true that the relation of master and slave and master and servant, for that matter, is one of mutual, though not equal, dependency. The relationship introduces a new structure into the polity and the social formation. *The Tempest* proposes an interestingly atavistic moment in history. It tacitly suggests the world where slavery began. There is no Europeanized history on this island until Prospero arrives; indeed there is hardly any human history at all, since the real mother of the slave is herself an import, 'hither brought with child/ And here was left by th'sailors.' (I, 2, 270–1)[9] Miranda, whose knowledge of society is formed in this peculiar community of violence, rage, and hatred, knows authority in the form of the subjection of the slave and the obedience of the daughter. She understands fear. And while her own fear of her father is a fear of being disobedient, she has the example of Caliban's real physical fear of frequently experienced physical pain before her. Her enticements to rebellion, that is, are circumscribed by dependency on her father for everything she requires. Caliban on the other hand, has no such motive for good behaviour. He has no function left but to serve Prospero and Miranda. He has no hopes of amelioration but their deaths or departures.

Caliban's sexual vitality is the primary source of his danger to Prospero and Miranda. The fear of rape is concomitant with the fear of the pollution of their species. Though nothing is said about Caliban's sexual organs, there is a way in which his own sexual knowledge makes his organs threatening, especially to European virginity. Coupled with the already current European mythology about the large and, even, grotesque sexual organs of non-white peoples (especially males), the assumptions about Caliban's sexuality fit comfortably into that aspect of the discourse of the play which constructs him as a savage object of fear and loathing.[10]

Like so many of the primitive peoples, described by Karen Newman, who formed part of the imaginations of sixteenth century Europeans, Caliban's clothing appears to be minimal.[11] This aspect of his persona is his master's way of demonstrating his primitivity and his dangerous, close-to-the-surface sexuality. In slave-owning societies, the slave's poverty meant that his or her clothes were meagre and inadequate. This very meagreness drew attention precisely to the very thing the clothes were designed to conceal – his or her sexuality: indeed, *déshabille*, a sexy feminine style of *un*dress, is an elegant and expensive imitation of poor dress. Caliban's 'gaberdine' is his loose garment which is capacious enough to accommodate himself and Trinculo, yet there is enough of his body visible to induce theorizing by the sailor about his species; there is no doubt, for example, in Trinculo's mind that the monster, fish or islander, is male – 'What have we here? A man or a fish? Dead or alive?' (II, 2, 25–6). It is virtually impossible to leave aside, in a consideration of Caliban, the issue of his monstrous sexuality, largely, of course, because it is a savage sexual desire that determines his outcast state. As we can still observe, images of bestiality were ubiquitous in the Renaissance. Pictures of centaurs and fauns, painted by male artists, were common. Common too, within them, was the idea of these mythical creatures using their potent animal sexuality both violently and merely seductively in pursuit of human women. Caliban's monstrosity belongs to the same category as those explosively sexual centaurs and fauns of Renaissance mythology.

Many writers on the play have not taken the issue of Caliban's sexual organs into account, but it seems to me that it is unlikely that they have not thought about the matter. After all, Caliban's deformity and monstrosity are constant subjects of attention, and it is perhaps noteworthy that Prospero can control him only through the use of supernatural power: that is to say, Caliban possesses physical strength sufficient in itself to intimidate his master. Though he is necessarily of human size, his conformations and deformations supply an image of something ugly and frightening to look at. Except for one sad and beautiful speech (III, 2, 137–45),[12] his language and action associate him with the aggressive physical body – what Bakhtin calls the 'grotesque body', or that aspect of physicality that has to do with the sexual and excretory functions.[13] The disgust he elicits in the Europeans indicates that the associations are rather automatic. Caliban's view of the Europeans, by contrast, is of cerebral beings who possess aggressive magic – invisible bullets – and that they will use them against him. His first words to Stephano are directly indicative: 'Do not torment me!' (II, 2, 56)

This inequality of response is a strong index of the power relationship. The universal disgust produced in the Europeans by Caliban's body is compelling evidence of his subjectability. The disgust indicates common agreement amongst them about his less than human identity, which, in turn, stands as a justification for their treatment of him. By contrast, the case of Othello is interestingly ambiguous. For a variety of reasons, and with several notable exceptions, the Venetians declare and demonstrate that they are *not* disgusted by Othello's body. Othello's body is like theirs, but slightly deformed in some details; and it is black. All but Brabantio, Iago, and Roderigo publicly give the impression that Othello's body does not disgust them. The assumption, however, that Othello is physically defective is nowhere more vividly shaped than when Desdemona says, as though it were the most natural thing in the world, that she saw Othello's visage in his mind. For others it seems frequently necessary to say aloud that they are not disgusted by Othello's body. The Duke, for example, allows that Othello's tale would win his daughter too. The duke is somewhat marginal in the play though central in the Venetian state; his daughter, however, is invisible. She is an allusion so shadowy that we must consider that the remark easily allows for the possibility that there is no daughter at all, that she is there for the sake of argument and illustration – and, as I have noted in Chapter 2, Othello is already safely married and out of the running for the Duke's daughter. Prospero and Miranda, on the other hand, are front and centre. Their treatment of Caliban is contingent on his proven and demonstrable species-inferiority and, above all, the sexual threat that his half-human body poses to them. Othello, at the start of the play, has already both proven his military value to the state as a protector and he has already invaded Venetian society and carried off one of its princesses. He is not subjectable, and therefore his body-difference is not made an object of political tyranny so long, in a sense, as he behaves like a white European man. However, the willingness to grant him the status of a human, which is so egregiously denied Caliban, is not universal. Even Othello's body evokes curiosity and questions.[14] To most he is, in considerably lesser degree than Caliban, a defective European.

Perhaps the most significant political fact about Caliban's body is that it is the site of violence. It is also, by logical extension, the site of struggle and resistance. That is, Prospero expresses aspects of himself on the body of his slave. He uses Caliban's body to inscribe his own power and Caliban's weakness. He enslaves him, confines him to a rock, uses him to supply necessaries to himself and his daughter, and causes his imps and spirits to punish and hurt Caliban's body. In each infliction of pain, Prospero makes his mastery felt. Caliban's body is the locus of the expression of that relation. Slavery, as we see here, is the physical power of a master over the body of his slave – the virtually complete ownership of that body and the ability to use it as he wishes. Caliban's capacity for resistance exists in his rebelliousness and even in his cries of pain which are themselves cries of anger and a kind of resistance to the inflictor of that pain. The cry of pain is a way of saying no.

That the play imbricates both the cruelty and the seductiveness of slavery is by now a truism of its criticism. That it furthermore constructs a stage in the discourse of colonialism is an equally important feature of more recent discussions. Paul Brown has adverted to this aspect of the play's political representation by pointing out that Caliban is 'nakedly enslaved to the master. The narrative of I.ii legitimises this exercise of power by representing Caliban's resistance to colonisation as the obdurate and irresponsible refusal of a simple educative project.'[15] And the habit of seeing Caliban not as a monster but as a colonized African or Indian has produced some remarkable and interesting constructions of the racial and imperial politics of the play.[16] But these seem to me starting points for an analysis of the use of the body of the slave by his owner and, also, for an interrogation of the relationship of the slave's body to the master's. Caliban is not just a black or brown man – that is to say a 'normal' or European man with a skin colour 'deficiency'. He, far more than Othello or Aaron, challenges the whole humanist project by being an actual monster, by possessing features and characteristics that are actual deformations of what is human. Hence the crucial importance of his body as an object that the European structures of political logic make it reasonable to loathe and subdue. For in that loathing and subduction lie one of the limitations of humanism. When we read about the benevolent treatment Caliban was given by Miranda and Prospero before his fall from their grace, we are really being told a story of dependency-creation which benefits the bestower. The 'kindness', 'humane care', 'goodness', 'pity', and 'pains' (I, 2, 347–59) which Prospero and Miranda lavished on Caliban in the early days were self-serving. At that time Caliban's body was an index or a site of their charity, a living confirmation of their goodness and capacity for nurture. His ultimate incapacity to remain passive and accept and receive the 'print of goodness'(I, 2, 354) ends up revealing the hollowness of the motive of his benefactors. The source of this goodness is equally the source of 'badness'. Failing to inscribe good on the body of Caliban, his masters simply switch tunes. Now he is imprinted with pain and suffering, pinches and stripes, tormented by those who once loved him. Clearly Prospero and Miranda gave their favours on the condition understood only by them. That goodness was bestowed only on condition that it produce gratitude, gratitude in a creature unable to understand the language of the bestowers.

Caliban's body natural is the foul and dreaded object of the play. It is an irrepressible and nature-bound pollutant on what has become Prospero's island, threatening contamination to all that is innocent and uncorrupted. Indeed, an ideology of innocence is a primary form in the oppressively enveloping political aesthetic of the tyrant of the isle. Innocence is a notion, a word that is valorized by Prospero as a condition and means of his mastery. Caliban's body and mind are not capable of conforming to this ideology and must therefore be suppressed by confinement and restraint. This perception of Caliban and his function is given heavy-handed symbolic force in the play by the monster's monstrosity. Ugly, malformed, odorous, Caliban's body is a constant presence, a reminder not of the political evil of the world of Europe, nor of the violence of the play's clowns and schemers, but of something deeper by far, some kind of grim and hideous depth in the human soul that cannot be exorcised or forgotten. Thus has been produced a self-evident conjunction in the European unconscious of Caliban and monstrosity. This is a connection which Caliban alone does not make. He is it; he is the symbolic presence of the excremental in life. The revulsion he arouses in the senses of his observers speaks to their unwilled recognition of and ambiguous relation to the constant embodied presence of the corruptive element.

The European body, epitomized in Ferdinand, apprehends the stranger's body, epitomized in Caliban, as a hateful thing. It is like and unlike his own body. But it is a manifestation of his own body which produces nausea in him. The body of an animal is easier to love than the body of a monster or an alien 'other'. The animal is *not* the self; the 'other' *is* the self. Caliban's body as a concept occupies a curious place in the imagination of his European tormentors as a nightmarish distortion of themselves. They are attracted and repelled by him. Closing in upon him, they seem, like Stephano and Trinculo, to be seeking in him a validation of their difference and superiority. Unhesitatingly and unquestioningly they and Prospero himself start acquaintance with a set of assumptions that entirely depend upon the subjugability of Caliban to themselves. They assume, correctly, their ability to compel submission in the monster. In Caliban's physical submission the Europeans recognize only his inferiority.

I have attempted, so far, to stay away from the question of racial hatred as it applies to the relation of Caliban to the Europeans. However, the issue has constantly asserted and reasserted itself throughout the writing of this chapter. The feelings of the Europeans towards Caliban resemble all too vividly the usual ('normal') feelings of white people towards black people. They are the feelings of nausea which Frantz Fanon uses to describe the encounter of the races – a kind of existential crisis of recognition.[17] Caliban will not go away. He nags at the consciousness of the Europeans without their being able to comprehend their own loathing. Colonialism is only part of the picture: Caliban belongs to Los Angeles in 1992 as much as to the colonized lands of Asia, Africa, and America in the seventeenth, eighteenth, and nineteenth centuries. European hatred of non-European, non-white people is in strong part fear and hatred of self. Caliban is merely a white person's version of that aspect of the self which it is acceptable to hate. It has taken the bloodless and jejune liberalism of the twentieth century – the tolerance and permission that has advanced capitalism, paternalism, and patriarchism – to produce utterly unuseful sympathy for Caliban, to consign him, that is, to a tender spot in the hearts of well-meaning people. And there he remains, an object of sympathy and charity and, because he is also ourselves, fear and hatred.

Notes

1. Growing up in South Africa, I was accustomed to the sight of 'ladies' and 'gentlemen' – as they loved to call themselves – bred in the very best English traditions of etiquette and good manners, transformed into truly terrifying fascists when they were displeased with their black servants. Miranda, here, though a potential rape victim, is very much in that mode.
2. Hayden White, 'The Forms of Wildness: Archaeology of an Idea', *The Wild Man Within: An Image in Western Thought from the Renaissance to Romanticism*, edited by Edward Dudley and Maximillian E. Novak (Pittsburgh: University of Pittsburgh Press, 1972), p. 15.
3. White, p. 15.
4. Richard Bernheimer, *Wild Men in the Middle Ages* (Cambridge: Harvard University Press: 1952), p. 2.
5. White, p. 36.
6. Stephen Greenblatt, 'Invisible bullets: Renaissance authority and its subversion, *Henry IV* and *Henry V*', *Political Shakespeare: new essays in cultural materialism*, edited by Jonathan Dollimore and Alan Sinfield (Ithaca: Cornell University Press, 1985), pp. 18–47.
7. Norman O. Brown, *Life Against Death: The Psychoanalytical Meaning of History* (New York: Vintage Books, 1959), p. 191.
8. Ibid.
9. Meridith Skura proposes that Ariel may have been the island's 'true reigning lord' when Sycorax arrived and promptly enslaved him, thus herself becoming the first 'colonialist, the one who established the habits of dominance and erasure before Prospero ever set foot on the island.' 'The Case of Colonialism in *The Tempest*', *Shakespeare Quarterly* 40 (1989), 46.
10. Karen Newman, '"And wash the Ethiop white': femininity and the monstrous in *Othello*', p. 148 and elsewhere.
11. Ibid.
12. On the basis of this speech, Stephen Orgel nominates Caliban 'the other great poet of the play'. He notes that while 'we see little enough of this side of Caliban, Prospero's fear and loathing render him utterly blind to it'. See 'Shakespeare and the Cannibals', *Cannibals Witches, and Divorce: Estranging the Renaissance*, Selected Papers from the English Institute, 1985; New Series, no. 11. Edited by Marjorie Garber (Baltimore: Johns Hopkins University Press, 1987), p. 57.
13. Mikhail Bakhtin, *Rabelais and His World*, translated by Helen Iswolsky (Cambridge: The M.I.T. Press, 1968), pp. 303–67.
14. In Jonathan Miller's BBC *Othello*, Othello, played by Anthony Hopkins,

is endowed with a gigantic codpiece in some kind of conformity with the stereotype which Miller ludicrously attempts both to negate and to exploit. Someone should have mentioned to him that a codpiece is not a sexual organ and the ability to wear a large codpiece belonged to each man in the play.

15. Paul Brown, '"This thing of darkness I acknowledge mine": *The Tempest* and the discourse of colonialism', *Political Shakespeare*, edited by Dollimore and Sinfield, p. 61.

16. For a comprehensive discussion of these, see Skura, 'Discourse and the Individual: The Case of Colonialism in *The Tempest'*.

17. Frantz Fanon, *Black Skin, White Masks*, translated by Charles Lam Markmann (New York: Grove Weidenfeld, 1967), especially Chapter Five, 'The Fact of Blackness', pp. 109–40.

Part II

5

Shakespeare's Poor:
2 *Henry VI*

The examples of Shylock, Othello, Caliban, and, later, Malvolio, all demonstrate the relative ease with which society can contain and control its marginalized individuals. Simply put, it gangs up on them, using the persuasive forces of socially sanctioned violence, scapegoating, and other ideological apparatuses by which the ruling class determines what is politically correct and what is not. Strangers and outsiders have little chance. In the case, however, of class animosities, there are significant differences. The ruling class has to control a collectivity of people which is larger than itself. It must dominate them but use the instruments of domination in less categorical ways than it uses them against easily separated individuals. One of the chief ways in which the poor are deromanticized, singled out, and controlled, is by ridicule and by being characterized as somehow 'in the wrong'. Poverty, like blackness or Jewishness, is a kind of defect.

The poor in Shakespeare's history plays receive short shrift. They tend to be violent, stupid, aggressive, vacillating, sycophantic, vicious, brutal and unkind. Though the rich and powerful are often no better, it is only in their ranks that we find a proportionate representation of complementary virtues. The poor appear to need the strong hand of patriarchal monarchy to provide them with moral and intellectual direction and purpose. Only infrequently do they cast up leaders from their ranks and, when they do, these leaders turn out to want, more than anything, to be like their masters, the rich and the royal. Poverty is indeed a curse in these plays, but it is as often as not represented as a curse on those who deserve it – a punishment for being poor. In representing the condition of poverty as a social and moral contagion, Shakespeare was, of course, perpetuating a truism of Western economic thought. Poverty in these plays is constructed by the author, but the construction is, as always, abetted by a vast complex of determinants including class and economics.

There have been some attempts to argue that Shakespeare's poor in the histories are ultimately sympathetically or, at best, ambivalently drawn. These attempts have tended to coincide with such upsurges of ideological and economic individualism as produced the scholarly works of Bradley, say, or those of Tillyard, Dover Wilson, and R. W. Chambers – periods when it was only with reluctance that ideological 'deficiencies' in Shakespeare were acknowledged. Thus, for example, R. W. Chambers attempts to argue in 'Shakespeare and the Play of *More*' that the poor of the histories (*2 Henry VI* in particular) are treated with genial and poetic sympathy but ultimately need the steady guiding hand of the powerful to achieve happiness. Chambers, almost elaborately, feels sorry for poor people, as his Shakespeare apparently did, and regards it as a mark of Shakespeare's superiority that he showed his sympathy for poverty in his plays.[1] There is at least one other and opposite way of regarding this alleged sympathy – as self-protective condescension. But within Chambers's world view, sympathy for the unfortunate is a moral rather than a political choice; it is a good or bad thing and not a decision about one's relation to society. With such sympathy and its concomitants and consequences – charity for example – the division between rich and poor can be justified within liberalism's moral framework by being ameliorable without threatening the economic structure. After making the claim for a sympathetic and compassionate poet, Chambers is obliged to identify himself and Shakespeare not with the poor but with the rich who judge them. Thus, the pauper demand for sufficient to eat is described by the critic in the terms in which they are presented in the play as 'false economics.'[2] The sympathy which Chambers detects in the plight of the poor is, apparently, sabotaged by an absurdity inherent to the poor and poverty, and discernible in 'the typical Shakespearean attitude to the mob. . . . These absurdities, depicted by the dramatist with fun and merry good humour, are, by a terrible combination, coupled with . . . merciless savagery.'[3]

Indeed, R. H. Tawney has argued powerfully that with the Reformation and the Protestant work ethic it was not long before poverty was regarded as a punishment for idleness and wealth as a reward for thrift and industry.[4] It is in large measure because so little compassion is expended on the poor by the rich in Shakespeare that Lear's 'Poor naked wretches' speech is regarded with so much admiration by Christian and Marxist critics alike, and almost everyone in between. The second tetralogy provides the best-known examples of poor and 'working class' characters, beggars and ill-paid working folk, whose plight remains unchanged in the end, and who remain, finally, in the very condition in which they first appeared. The would-be leaders amongst them end up discomfited by the conservative forces of a self-sustaining and self-referential patriarchal politics. The leaders who end up leading the poor are drawn from the aristocracy and nobility. Thus, to cite one well-used example, Prince Hal is far more popular with the poor than Falstaff, who is virtually, if anomalously, one of them. The tavern-folk of *Henry IV 1* and *2* include the notorious Francis who supplies so much amusement to the prince and whose plight inspired G. L. Kittredge's lofty observation that 'Sentimental readers . . . need not distress themselves. When Francis grew up and became an innkeeper himself, we may be sure that he often told with intense satisfaction how he had once been on intimate terms with Prince Hal.'[5] Michael Bristol has evaluated this impulse of both drama and criticism to neutralize and disarm plebeian dissatisfaction with the ruling class. But, he notes, a 'wish to discourage or ignore manifestations of popular culture will not of itself cause that culture to disappear.'[6] Plebeian culture has been attacked and diminished by the potent literary weapon of ridicule. It is simply not a serious alternative to present rule in the minds of bourgeois dramatists and their audiences and critics. Sympathy for the lot of the poor is a very different thing from letting them take their plight into their own hands. Unless the remedy is seen to lie within the power of their rulers, the dominant culture's helplessness has to be acknowledged. This was and is unthinkable to the adherents of that culture.

Commentary and criticism have been complicit in such constructions of Shakespeare's weak and working class. They are known as the low characters, the farce characters, the fools, the butts, the knaves and whores. One might consider the various critical celebrations of Feeble (*2 Henry IV*), who declares that he will fight for his king because we 'owe God a death'(III,2,230). This simple, straightforward and courageous remark has elicited disproportionate praise from generations of bourgeois critics and audiences because its source has been deemed so unlikely – Feeble is a rural working man who possesses a valiant mind – and because every other impressed citizen seems to be aware of how small his stake will be in the victory of either side in the dispute and would rather go home than fight. Why Feeble has any interest in fighting on behalf of the illegal and corrupt monarchy is one of the great unasked questions of Shakespeare criticism. Why the critics have been so delighted by his exhibition of patriotic loyalty to his monarch is less difficult to understand. Shakespeare studies have, perhaps until recently, overwhelmingly been the preserve of middle-class, liberal and conservative practitioners whose values are vividly expressed in such things as the admiration for Feeble's loyalty to his monarch, a loyalty that plainly and simply opts for an entrenched monarchical order. The very absence of critical self-consciousness about how patronizing the critics have sounded in this praise is itself an index of how offensive it really is. The theatre too has, for the most part, supported this kind of characterization or construction, though it would be unfair to neglect the many honourable exceptions to this generalization. A number of well-known Shakespeare productions have, indeed, hinged upon powerful and sympathetic representations of the poor. Yet, there remains substantial truth in Margot Heinemann's remark that 'in modern productions these characters are routinely presented as gross, stupid and barely human – rogues, sluts and varlets with straw in their hair, whose antics the audience can laugh at but whose combination of Loamshire dialect and dated jokes often makes the comments unintelligible anyway.'[7] This kind of pre-sentation will be familiar. Poverty on the Shakespeare stage is mainly – though not inevitably – comic. Poor people are made to sound funny; their accents and their mangling of what we are taught to understand as The English Language are a prime source of humour; their wit, while often effective and wise, is devalued by being unrefined and inelegant. Their clothes, often mere rags, and a scutcheon of their wearer's social worthlessness, are also a frequent source of humour (it is sometimes forgotten that the stylized diamond pattern on Harlequin's costume is a carryover from his older *commedia dell'arte* humorous costume of tatters and patches).[8] Peasants are a staple of laughter in Renaissance art, Stephen Greenblatt affirms, while he reminds us of the distinction between Rabelaiseian shared laughter that stresses the crossing of social boundaries, and Sidneian laughter that underscores social differences.[9] It is the unavoidable practice of Shakespeare's plays that they represent the 'rich' as normal, and the poor as abnormal – though it has been argued that rational economic and sociological reasons determined this bias. Indeed, notwithstanding the fact that the poor population of Shakespeare's England vastly outnumbered the rich and the comfortable, it is a feature of the plays that the poor person is represented as a defective rich person. This representation is made the more normal by the fact that the dearest wish of the poor person is almost always to *be* a rich person.

The disproportionate characterizations of rich and poor are contingent on historical forces that have created the unequal distribution of wealth and power and force them to succumb to these distortions of presentation. Though the poor hugely outnumbered the rich, the contingencies of urban life and the economics of the theatre produced a false picture of the real proportions – as it undoubtedly does in theatre today where the poor are notable for their absence, both onstage and in the audience. In real life the poor would have been almost everywhere *except* in the court and the theatre, which both would have functioned as refuges for the wealthy from the normally ubiquitous poverty. Poverty in the midst of plenty is always a threat to plenty, and it is reasonable to regard the theatre as a culturally validated means of defusing that threat through ridicule, sentimentality, or demonization. Theatre audiences have usually included only a minority of the poor; the plays reinforce the notion of the harmlessness of poverty by similarly including only a minority of – usually risible or dangerous – poor amongst their *dramatis personae*.

Class hatred is given powerful play in *2 Henry VI*. All classes are represented as profoundly flawed, and hopelessly corrupt. The nobility is reckless, power-crazed, divided within itself. It is torn by the wranglings of ambitious people who have within their grasps the possibility of tyrannical power. The poor are quasi-comic in their villainous lust for wealth and power, and simply and utterly stupid in their notions of how to use either. Their means of achieving power are brutal and savage. Their sheer 'otherness' in the England of the play is that of dark, strange, bestial foreigners from whom the rest of society needs protection. The middle class, represented by the minor politicians like the Mayor of Saint Albans, and such functionaries as the Clerk of Chatham, are nervous, pusillanimous presences who are, however, concerned about national political and social stability in ways that seem not to touch the warring nobles and peasantry.

2 Henry VI is an interesting study in rich–poor relations particularly because amongst the rich and powerful there is such intense and nasty dissension and disagreement that the stability of the hierarchy is in constant danger of collapse. The parties are various, the divisions are multiple, and rancour lurks on every side. The king himself is an impotent weakling and his wife loves a noble who is killed not by a friend of the king but by one of his enemies. Duke Humphrey seems immobilized by his overweening sense of himself and his honour, and it is a relief when he is killed. The queen is faithful only to power and ambition. Political stability, that is, and moral direction are virtually absent amongst the powerful; this becomes especially true after the deaths of the Duke of Gloucester and Lord Say who had possessed some potential moral leadership. And yet, for all that rage and murderous hatred are pervasive within the ruling class, the poor and the working people are seen as so many fools and dolts, easily misled by a villain who promises them anarchy, wealth, and revenge against their enemies, the rich. But they are equally capable of fighting for the king merely because they are exhorted to do so. John Cade, the leader of the only revolution of the poor in Shakespeare, is seen by the nobles as a violent, vicious and ambitious villain; this perception of Cade is almost unanimously shared by critics and audiences alike, deriving from some incontestable brutalities and lies he commits. But it derives as well from the fact that he is supported and encouraged by the poor, those whose interests are in precise opposition to those of playmakers, audiences, and critics through the ages.

Cade threatens revolution, upheaval, bloodshed and civil war – if, that is, you are on the other side of him. To that side it is axiomatic that he must be exterminated, and when he is killed by Alexander Iden, the rhetorical forces of drama conspire in word, action, and verse to imply that his death is a decidedly good thing. Yet, to the poor he is a serious political figure who is willing, and who sees the need, to use violence to effect political change. The play tends to ridicule the potential seriousness of his challenge to monarchy by belittling his followers and falling back automatically onto the stereotyping discussed above. The drama (the playwright?) discredits him before he appears onstage. He is not given the chance to seem the revolutionary hero that many of his followers would have celebrated. The Duke of York discloses, for example, that far from being an independent rebel with a cause, Cade is really in his pay, hired to stir up strife and dissension in the kingdom, 'To make commotion, as full well he can / Under the title of John Mortimer.'(II,1,358–9) He is, in other words, a false pretender to the throne. But when Cade gets up some steam of his own, he shows an ideology that has less to do with his claim to the throne than with an awareness of the needs and aspirations of the poor, which are characteristically mocked. Cade promises his followers,

> your captain is brave and vows reformation. There shall be in England seven half-penny loaves sold for a penny; the three-hoop'd pot shall have ten hoops; and I will make it felony to drink small beer. All the realm shall be in common, and in Cheapside shall my palfrey go to grass. And when I am king, as king I will be, –
> *All.* God save your Majesty!
> *Cade.* I thank you, good people – there shall be no money; all shall eat and drink on my score, and I will apparel them all in one livery, that they may agree like brothers, and worship me their lord.
> *Butcher.* The first thing we do, let's kill all the lawyers.
>
> (IV, 2, 62–73)

It is well and interestingly documented by Robert Darnton that old peasant fairy tales often hinge on the provision of a good square meal as the dearest wish of the subject;[10] to the poor peasants of fairy tales, magic alone is capable of providing such extravagances as a sufficiency of meat and drink on demand. The crowd in this passage who hail Cade as their king are represented as ingenuous fools who believe in magic. Their belief in the possibility of enough food becoming available by merely changing rulers is represented as the height of naïveté. Their credulity is mocked at the same time that their hunger is given focus. This discontinuity in the text – almost a contradiction as audience sympathy and ridicule are uncomfortably conjoined – supplies a moment of disruption in the smooth flow of mockery of the poor. It is not possible or necessary to determine which impulse is uppermost in the text – that is, are they more fools than hungry or more hungry than fools? It is, however, important to see that the two needs expressed here coexist dependently because of a political system in which suppressions create their own resistances. The desire for a benevolent monarch is expressed in the clamour for Cade who will, he says, grant wishes. The fantasy of unlimited food and drink means in this context simply the absence of hunger. Michael Bristol is too literal-minded in his dismissal of the logic of 'seven half-penny loaves sold for a penny'; he sees numbers where he ought to see words. A 'half-penny loaf' describes not a price but a thing, a loaf of bread of a certain size and weight. It costs a half-penny, Cade could be saying, but it ought to cost a seventh of a penny.[11]

So deep-rooted is individualism as a means to independence and freedom that a Cade – or for that matter, a Falstaff in another context – can only conceive of liberation through the acquisition of power within the existing framework of monarchy. And yet, even within the hopeless fantasy with which Cade attempts to deceive his followers, there is a notable difference. For although Cade wishes to be worshipped as a lord, he proposes an unusual kind of community of his worshippers. The abolition of money is to be accompanied by a sufficiency of the necessaries of life and a single livery for all to designate the brotherhood and equality of those beneath him. One must not make too much of this fantasy as an economic and political policy, though it bears a rather uncanny resemblance to certain totalitarian dictatorships of the twentieth century as well as strikingly anticipating some of the communal economic and political ambitions and programmes of the Diggers and Levellers of the mid-seventeenth century.[12] However, Cade's depiction of political happiness strikes directly at the failure of the patriarchal monarchy to supply contentment. It is of course clear that Cade's notions are represented as ludicrous; and the sight of this megalomaniac being prematurely hailed as 'Majesty' by a credulous mob is designed to discredit both the majesty and the mob. But at the same time the sheer want expressed in the enthusiasm for the idea of enough to eat and drink is itself a subversion of what is. That men need a leader is a given of the political plays; that a leader will inevitably, therefore, emerge from amongst men is an equally unquestioningly held belief.

The evident illegitimacy of Cade as a leader rests on a number of factors, such as his palpably false claim to the throne and his subornation by York. However, we have seen such things often enough in Shakespeare, and we have seen equally fraudulent claims to the throne succeed or nearly succeed. No, what really discredits Cade is his poverty. He is separated from real power by a class system that is so rigidly inscribed into the political dogmas of the play as to be ultimately insuperable. Within the text, Cade has no means of escaping from the language, manners, and habits that have made him or the followers who are tainted in the same way. Within the supertext or intertext – that body of customs and prejudices which determine and are determined by the surrounding political and cultural networks that have nurtured the play through history and, as well, Cade in his incarnation as a villain – Cade is defeated by the bourgeois conventions of comedy. His rough, ugly violence is rough and ugly because of his class and the class of his followers and manipulators. Part of what makes Cade a *dramatically implausible* monarch is the prospect of him in social and political control of the aristocracy. This is a prospect which is implicit in everything he does and says, but its absurdity is ideological, not inevitable. Dick the Butcher's immortal 'The first thing we do, let's kill all the lawyers', (IV, 2, 73) is one of the best remembered and funniest lines in the canon because it expresses a fantasy in terms of the purest comic exaggeration. It is also one of those rare jokes that transcend class by constructing in hyperbolical fashion the truism that lawyers are themselves a class and are the enemy of everyone in society regardless of social standing. But part of its humour lies in the class of the person who says the line. He really means it, and we are prepared to laugh at him because of the sheer, lovely, mad naïveté of the sentiment. The very modesty of Cade's promises is comic – seven half-penny loaves for a penny – because it refers to a way of life that accepts poverty as well-earned, and alleviation as simple yet beyond reality. The idea of a monarch promising a chicken in every pot is not humorous because in some way the monarch's authority is sufficient to realize the fantasy. Cade's promise of virtually free bread and drink is comical because it is removed from reality by virtue of who Cade is: the fantasy is discredited by the traditional relation of comedy and poverty.

While bourgeois plays like this one construct poverty as comic by exploiting class differentiation, so violence is constructed as class-referential. The violence of the poor, like the violence of the rich, can take many forms. But, amongst the rich, violence is more complex and is more complexly imbricated into the social fabric. Unlike the poor, the rich are able to perform acts of violence that can purify and dignify the social formation. They can also, of course, do the opposite: the rich can participate in acts of violence that cause disharmony and social discontinuity, as amply evidenced in *2 Henry VI*. Amongst the poor, however, violence usually lacks the political direction and determination perceptible as the basis of violence amongst the rich who, having money, want to stabilize their wealth by additional power. Acts of violence by the poor in the histories are denigrated and ridiculed by their actual remoteness from the reaches of real power. A man who would overthrow his monarch for the sake of bread is represented as clottish, while the man who would overthrow the monarch in order to assume the monarch's power is aggrandized as menacing, evil, ambitious, proud. In this play the outrageous stupidity of the poor is exposed in their manipulability, their easily broken alliances, their unreliability, and their greed. What might, in another context, be characterized as the deliberate product of their hopeless and tragic dependency on the rich, is here mocked as mental and psychological weakness. When in Act IV, scene 8 Old Clifford appeals to his 'countrymen', the Cade rabblement, to follow the king rather than Cade, they obligingly cry 'God save the King!'(19) Minutes later they are acclaiming Cade again: 'We'll follow Cade, we'll follow Cade!'(33) One stirring speech further on and the clamour is for 'A Clifford! a Clifford! we'll follow the King and Clifford.'(54)

Violence itself is a politically constructed concept in the plays. There are the violent acts of the rich and the violent acts of the poor. The violence of the rich and powerful is always hedged with a rhetoric of righteousness, with the anxious claim that it is necessary for the good of society – however phony that claim proves to be. The examples of Hal and Hotspur will stand out. To Hal the killing of Hotspur is an act of purification and vindication; his language declares his purpose. He promises his father not merely to strike down his enemy, but to stain his favours in a bloody mask. Hotspur too, justifies his violence on equally grandiose lines. *2 Henry VI* is no exception to this habit of partiality. Even the brutal manner of Suffolk's death declares his own magnificent courage in a way that is typical of the violent deaths of many a noble villain. His last words insist on the importance and meaning of his life:

> Come, soldiers, show what cruelty ye can,
> That this my death may never be forgot.
> Great men oft die by vile bezonians.
> A Roman sworder and banditto slave
> Murder'd sweet Tully; Brutus' bastard hand
> Stabb'd Julius Caesar; savage islanders
> Pompey the Great; and Suffolk dies by pirates.

> (IV, 1, 132–8)

Cade's career, on the other hand, is represented as one lurch from random, violent destruction to the next. He is engaged in an orgy of killing that shows no sign of letting up. It is, of course, politically expedient for the dominant culture to represent the forces that threaten it in the light of chaotic and mad destruction, but where Shakespeare's plays fit into the progress of that culture is a complex question. For example, do they advance these stereotyped notions or do they interrogate them? Do the poor in his plays – and in this one in particular – conform to the idea of them held by the rich or that held by the poor, or both? Are our criteria for evaluating and analyzing the construction of poverty and violence those fostered by the plays, our own notions and ideologies, Shakespeare's own, or those of the histories of poverty and violence over the last four centuries? The best answer to these questions is all of the above. For indeed it is not possible to perceive stage violence without reference to a knowledge of actual violence. And that knowledge will have been determined by a great multiplicity of ordinary experiences shaped by psychological, cultural, historical, literary, philosophical and religious forces in our lives.

The uniqueness of *2 Henry VI* is in the fact that this is Shakespeare's only play in which the political structure of patriarchal monarchy is actually threatened, is almost destroyed. In other plays that structure is endangered by those who would replace the monarch – we might think of the possibility of a Falstaff as the nation's Lord Chief Justice, for example – but here the spectre of the rule of the poor and disadvantaged is presented seriously. The established order undergoes its greatest challenge. John Cade and his 'rabblement' (they are decidedly not freedom fighters or, even, soldiers) actually defeat contingents of legitimate soldiers and frighten the established authority by raising the alarm of a revolution. This is a cultural and historical possibility that is treated with considerable anxiety in Shakespeare's political plays. The demonization of the poor in these plays is no less, and no less complex than, the demonization of other marginalized social entities in the other plays – Jews, blacks, women. Like those other marginal types, the poor are endowed with qualities that make them unincorporable into the mainstream of power politics. By definition they are 'wrong' or deformed, and incapable of being absorbed into the echelon of the dominant authority.

Though the poor always do and always will outnumber the rich, because the rich possess wealth and its concomitants, power, authority, and control of literacy, it is they who get to define and theorize poverty. Hence a poor person takes on the persona of a defective rich person in the cultural languages of middle-class societies. Endued with qualities that are inherently comic, according to bourgeois standards and traditions, they are disqualified from true leadership. Cade, we need to recall, is always operating under the secret aegis of the Duke of York. Comedy, we might remember, is synonymous with an underdeveloped moral sense in this play. The histories raise a very important related question in which something of an answer to the dilemma of poverty as moral degradation is offered. Why is it that the noble forces opposing the monarchy – those of the Lancasters, the Percies, the Plantagenets, the Nevils etc. – are represented as plausible (though not always desirable) alternative governments to those of the standing monarchies while the poor who would assume power are represented as megalomaniacal and absurd? And how are these representations accomplished?

In those situations in which the rich would overthrow the monarch, it is always the case that they and the threatened monarch share the common economic interest of wealth, which is denied the large mass of people. All contestants in such conflicts wish to maintain a feudal social structure which is sharply and deeply divided along lines of power and powerlessness, or wealth and poverty. At no time do the pretenders to the throne offer a redistribution of wealth – as we have seen Cade do in his promise to alleviate hunger. The powerful all want one thing – more power – and they see the means to that increase in power and wealth in the monarchy itself. Hence a myriad spurious and not so spurious claims to a monarchy that has anyway been so often disjoined in history that a pure lineage no longer exists. All claimants to the throne are following old precedent, as Richard II fully recognizes in his speech on the history of violence in his own monarchy – 'all murdered'. They want, in other words, to maintain a hierarchical economic structure with themselves at the top, for the sake of which the present monarch must be removed, normally by violence. For such a structure to survive, as the depressing conclusion of *King Lear* indicates – at least in Jonathan Dollimore's reading of it[13] – the poor need to remain in a permanent condition of want. The claims of these nobles on the poor whom they will or do govern are themselves interesting. Never do they offer the poor redress of their poverty though they acknowledge them *as* the poor in a variety of ways. They offer them stability, friendship, even in the case of Henry V, brotherhood ('this little band of brothers'); they doff their bonnets to oyster wenches, but their poverty and their place in the hierarchy is understood to be fixed. This, of course, is not news in itself. But, in the context of the Cade uprising, it is extremely interesting. Cade, unlike Shakespeare's other contenders for the crown, offers them a new society, though he is damned for it in every conceivable dramatic form.[14]

The violent means of the noble pretenders always propose a predictable and known end. Though Duke Humphrey is hideously and brutally murdered, the purpose of his murder is to install a monarch who will command a monarchy that a patriarchally-oriented society will be familiar with. There will in this and other such cases – Richard III and Macbeth, for example – be a monarch whose hold on power will remain contingent upon the unequal division of wealth and power and whose loss of power in no way disturbs this basic economic reality. Cade is a menacing anomaly because he offers no certainty. His case provokes a certain anxiety, reflected in the text in large measure by the unpredictable consequences his success would produce. But his solution to the economic woes of his followers threatens the entire economic structure by which the monarchy exists. Cade, in his rather crude way, is offering communism to his followers. It is indeed an undeveloped and untheorized communism, but essential to it is the promise of state-supported and financed sufficiency of food and drink – to each according to his needs. Of course, the notion is treated with ridicule; its sheer pie-in-the-sky lunacy is foregrounded, so that it is made to seem little more than a mad joke. But we, unlike Shakespeare, live in a world in which such programmes and platforms, occasionally no more articulate or sophisticated than Cade's, have facilitated the overthrow of oligarchies in various parts of the world. But Cade is discredited from the start as the hero of a radical revolution bent on change. He is directed by York. He bases his credibility as a leader on a specious claim to high birth – his father was a Mortimer, he claims, his mother a Plantagenet – in doing which he valorizes the principle of lineal succession. And his sheer lying crudeness, ridiculed even by his followers, makes him into an essentially unserious threat to the monarchy of Henry.

Cade's promise of food and drink in large and cheap supply further undermines his leadership. The idea is marked as preposterous and leads directly to the fantasy of killing all the lawyers.

This notion interestingly incorporates the lawyers as a class, as a recognizable obstacle to the freedom of the poor, and enables Cade to sidestep the role of the aristocracy in suppressing the poor. What follows from the threat to kill the lawyers is a maniacal orgy of revenge against other cultural institutions which are seen as oppressive. The Clerk of Chatham is brought before the rebels and sent to execution largely on the grounds that he is able to read and write. Such rough justice, of course, is shocking to a middle-class audience schooled in the values of literacy. Perhaps it is more shocking to us today, who are all literate, than it might have been to societies in which literacy was the exception rather than the rule; hard, violent societies where reading and writing were justifiably regarded as the means to power accessible only to the few, rather than to the many. Annabel Patterson has noted that the attack on literacy is a 'primitivist defence of the old crafts against mechaniza-tion . . . blurred by a negative focus on language skills as an evil science [which] gives place . . . to the connection between educa-tional disparity and unequal access to legal justice'.[15] A man who, like the Clerk of Chatham, can write, possesses in such societies a secret and privileged means to power; he is then reasonably re-garded as an object of suspicion. The notion that literacy is avail-able to all, within the means of the whole society, and that the power it supplies is open and accessible, is a very modern notion. We make a mistake to ridicule the murder of a man on the grounds that he is literate, for it is a tragically serious act, much imitated in modern history. We ought to understand more quickly, perhaps, than the benighted followers of Cade, the real and immense and potentially tyrannical power of writing. Certainly this power has been well understood by those dictators in our own century who have burned books. That act is, in a way, the greatest act of deference to the power of a book.

The desire to kill all the lawyers and the actual execution of the Clerk of Chatham by a mob of working poor are themselves elo-quent expressions of the degree of alienation of the poor from the positions of power. There is a way of reading these moments in the play as a warning against the rule of the mob. If the mob had its way, the argument goes in this play and insistently in the two parts of *Henry IV*, there would be poor people in power. This by defini-tion would mean a rule of scum, ruffians, criminals, dirty, dis-honest, envious people with no sense of social good. The plays proliferate with metaphors, emanating from the echelons of power, which combine to suggest that the laws of nature itself have ordained that political power belongs to the rich and the noble; any attempt to reverse or invert this law, according, let it be noted, to those who design the metaphors, will lead to social catastrophe in which all members of society will suffer. The mad and murderous career of Cade is so constructed as to suggest this law in action. We are shown the injustice, the perversion of values, the lying, and the random cruel violence to which the Cades of this world and their followers are particularly prone. These followers, interestingly, all have trades – they are a working class. But they are the embodiment of the many admonitions Henry IV gives his son.

So much is easy. However, it is important to recognize that this text resists such simplicity of interpretation by constantly, though not very obviously or deliberately, displacing the finality of such judgements onto the opposing forces of disturbance in the social formation. The dominant paternal authority of the play is in a state of high disarray. Conflict and sabotage are normal; the warring factions of the rich and powerful are all bent on controlling the hapless monarch. There are significant ways in which this intestine intra-class warfare differs from the strife in the ranks of the poor. When the rich fight they virtually disregard the poor as subjects in their struggles. To them the poor are mere pawns or instruments in the achievement of their ambitions. To the poor, on the other hand, the rich are the impediment itself to their access of power. Thus, the transgressive energy that expresses itself among the poor is doubly illegitimate. For, as the rich renegade or traitor might wish to overthrow the monarch, he needs to be able to reassure a significant portion of the nobility of his need of them and of his determination to bolster their own power. He can succeed only if he can convince his powerful and aristocratic allies of his devotion to the law that has sustained them to this point. Thus, of course, much of the political wrangling in all the political plays is around the very complex and indeterminate issue of legitimacy. All sides within the aristocratic communities claim legitimacy. The poor, by contrast, throw the whole notion of legitimacy into question. They cannot succeed in their quest for power by adhering to the laws, as the rich constantly argue they can. The fear expressed in the desire to kill all the lawyers and in the execution of the Clerk of Chatham underscores the authority that the written word and the letters of the law represent to the poor.

Cade's nemesis is Alexander Iden, used by Shakespeare to put a full stop to the rebellion without compromising the values of *noblesse oblige*. Phyllis Rackin and, to a lesser extent, Stephen Greenblatt have examined the implications of Iden's class and his motive for murder. He is not an aristocrat fighting the rebels and protecting the interests of power and wealth: on the contrary, he is a country gentleman protecting his property and his person from a thief who aggressively threatens his life – 'Nay, it shall ne'er be said, while England stands,/ That Alexander Iden, esquire of Kent,/ Took odds to combat a poor famish'd man.'(IV, 10, 41–3). Rackin argues that 'Shakespeare's representation of Iden's act and his character rationalizes a new source of status, the ownership of private property, in the emblems of an older world'. She notes that 'Cade is finally reduced to a mechanism for ideological containment. Shakespeare's representation of Cade invokes the stereotypes of murdering thief and comic villain, the first to project and the second to defuse the anxieties of privileged property owners.'[16]

The dialogue between George Bevis and John Holland amusingly highlights some of the sources of the discontent in the underclass. But like most such social criticism, this is neutralized by virtue of the comic language in which it is couched. In another context the satire might be telling, striking as it does at the inequities of class; yet once again the moral wisdom of the poor is made the substance of easy humour:

> *Holland.* Well I say it was never merry world in England since gentlemen came up.
> *Bevis.* O miserable age! Virtue is not regarded in handicraftsmen.
> *Holland.* The nobility think scorn to go in leather aprons.
> (IV, 2, 6–14)

The significant dividing line between classes in the play is literacy itself. The poor attack the rich for their ability to read and for their control of the instruments of literacy. In his condemnation of Lord Say, Cade accuses him among other things of 'traitorously corrupt-[ing] the youth of the realm in erecting a grammar-school. . . . It will be proved thou has men about thee that usually talk of a noun, and a verb, and such abominable words as no Christian ear can endure to hear.'(IV, 7, 30–8) The connections between literacy and the law and the law and oppression is given shape in Cade's command: 'Away! burn all the records of the realm; my mouth shall be the parliament of England.'(IV, 7, 12–4) Few moments in the play more vividly contribute to the demonization of the poor. The spectacle of a nearly successful leader of a peasant revolt bent upon the destruction of the civilization is not pretty. The construction of the fickle mob of handicraftsmen and peasants as potential rulers makes the mad violent hijinks around the throne seem tame. But, as we easily slide into the wholesale condemnation of the philistines who would destroy the records of our civilization, we might do well to consider the many ways in which the fear of literacy is justified, and how literacy itself has been an instrument of the oppression. For this play confirms the relationship of wealth and literacy, and, by extension, of power and literacy, and consequently of morality and literacy. For morality, like the other ideological formations, is defined and controlled by those who articulate cultural norms.

Notes

1. R. W. Chambers, 'Shakespeare and the Play of *More*', *Man's Unconquerable Mind: Studies in English Writers, from Bede to A. E. Housman and W. P. Ker* (London: Jonathan Cape, 1939), pp. 204–49.
2. Chambers, p. 216.
3. Chambers, p. 218.
4. R. H. Tawney, *Religion and the Rise of Capitalism: A Historical Study* (Gloucester, Mass.: Peter Smith, 1962), pp. 227–75.
5. Admiringly quoted by J. Dover Wilson in *The Fortunes of Falstaff* (Cambridge: Cambridge University Press, 1964), p. 49.
6. Michael D. Bristol, *Carnival and Theater: Plebeian Culture and the Structure of Authority in Renaissance England* (New York: Methuen, 1985), p. 45.
7. Margot Heinemann, 'How Brecht read Shakespeare', *Political Shakespeare*, edited by Dollimore and Sinfield, p. 225.
8. Kenneth M. Cameron and Theodore J. C. Hoffman, *The Theatrical Response* (London: Macmillan, 1969), p. 138.
9. Stephen Greenblatt, 'Murdering Peasants: Status, Genre, and the Representation of Rebellion', *Learning to Curse: Essays in Modern Culture* (New York: Routledge, 1990), p. 116.
10. Robert Darnton, *The Great Cat Massacre and Other Episodes in French Cultural History* (New York: Basic Books, 1984), pp. 32–4.
11. Bristol, p. 89. Bristol's literal reading of this line is typical. To Greenblatt, and most other critics besides, the sheer bufoonery of Shakespeare's rebels is exemplified by this apparently illogical promise. See 'Murdering Peasants', *Learning to Curse*, p. 124.
12. Christopher Hill, *The Century of Revolution: 1603–1714* (London: Nelson, 1961).

13. Jonathan Dollimore, *Radical Tragedy: Religion, Ideology and Power in the Drama of Shakespeare and his Contemporaries* (Chicago: University of Chicago Press, 1984), pp. 189–202.

14. For a description of the background to the pre-1640 class hostility and the movements to which it referred, see Christopher Hill, *The World Turned Upside Down: Radical Ideas during the English Revolution* (London: Temple Smith, 1972), especially pp. 11–46.

15. Annabel Patterson, *Shakespeare and the Popular Voice* (Oxford: Basil Blackwell, 1989), p. 49.

16. Phyllis Rackin, *Stages of History: Shakespeare's English Chronicles* (Ithaca: Cornell University Press, 1990), p. 216. In 'Murdering Peasants' Greenblatt proposes that in this scene status relations 'are being transformed before our eyes into property relations, and the concern . . . for maintaining social and even cosmic boundaries is reconceived as a concern for maintaining freehold boundaries. Symbolic estate gives way to real estate.' (p. 125)

6

To Have Not: *King Lear* and Money

The opening scene of *King Lear* grinds with the harsh music of money. From the first line of that scene to the last, money or trade dominates the interests of all involved. Even Cordelia, against her will, is forced to point out to her father that she owes him and her husband-to-be half (fifty per cent) each of her sum of love. Notwithstanding the emphasis on wealth and the monetary value of things, the word *gold*, a typical synonym for wealth, is used only twice in the play. By intriguing contrast, it is used thirty-seven times in *Timon of Athens* where its metaphorical value as an index of possessions and poverty is given full play. In *Lear*, division refers to a division of wealth, of money, of property, of possessions. Gold won't do; as a substance it is too remote from experience and too mythologically connotative for the purposes of this drama. We need to hear, and the king's subjects need to see on a map and hear, the evaluative details of

> bounds, even from this line to this,
> With shadowy forests and with champains rich'd,
> With plenteous rivers and wide-skirted meads

> (I, 1, 62–4)

The bases of the divisions have to do with the relation of wealth to morality and the use of wealth as a moral measure. Indeed the idea of *measure* comes, contradictorily, to seem one of the chief means of sustaining a social and economic system of inequality. The notion supports an ideology of sufficiency, excess, and, naturally, insufficiency. As this play demonstrates, not having enough is worse than having nothing. Too little to eat, too little to wear, too little to live on, are the conditions of beggary. Nothingness, by contrast, and because it is abstract and metaphorical, is fantastical, surreal. Cordelia's 'nothing' emerges out of excessive and violent

73

psychological struggle. Her speech, in which she explains her 'nothing', is really a plea for the value of moderation. And moderation has to do with much, little, and enough. Moderation is as culturally determined a concept as excess; but it is a value that is likelier to find sympathy in a *Lear* audience than is the value of excess.

The social order of *King Lear* reflects these imbalances in possession. The wars are fought, however, not between the poor and the rich, but between the rich and the rich; and this is the usual way. Most wars are of this kind: those in power wage war against others with power while they both use the powerless as their engines of battle. There is a logical, even natural enmity between those who have and those who do not have; despite this fact of opposing interests, it is seldom in human history that actual wars are fought between these two groups – such a phenomenon, anyway, is called a revolution, not a war, and usually takes the form of an intestine civil conflict between classes rather than between one nation pitted against another or two power interests fighting for the same position within a nation. The play produces the conditions for a civil revolt of the poor against their masters and keepers. It shows a world of cruelty and indifference and class hatred in which the poor are helpless against the rich. Poverty in the play is shown as a form of deprivation whose conditions are isolation, want, and weakness. But, for all that the plight of the poor is foregrounded, there is no threat to stability from that segment or class of the society of *King Lear*.

War, paradoxically, is a kind of reverse conspiracy of the rich to maintain the rule of the rich. When powers contend in Shakespeare there are always clear understandings between them, however unstated they may be. Chief of all these unspoken agreements is that the outcome of the war will merely be substitutive rule – one set of rich and powerful people will possess the power, whether they are the set who held power before the war or the set to replace them. It is clearly understood by the rich that the nation's good is synonymous with the unequal distribution of wealth. For social stability to be maintained, it is always understood by the dominant interest that there must be a minority of rich and a majority of poor people. The political crux of the drama of *King Lear* is the war between France and England. It is a war of curious ambiguity as it mixes up loyalties and allegiances in an audience, though not, evidently in the characters of the play.

Cordelia is represented in some odd way to be on the wrong side, fighting for France against Britain. There is no serious alternative to her defeat and, concomitantly, that of France. The promise Cordelia holds for Britain may be of a fairer rule than that which obtains, a rule of right and decency, but only under a French monarch. Nowhere, however, is there promise made of a redistribution of power and wealth. The potential rule of France and Cordelia offers nothing in the way of the amelioration of poverty. Jonathan Dollimore has argued: 'as their world disintegrates Lear and Gloucester cling even more tenaciously to the only values they know, which are precisely the values which precipitated the disintegration. Hence even as society is being torn apart by conflict, the ideological structure which has generated that conflict is being reinforced by it.'[1]

The first scene has all the components of dishonesty, corruption, sycophancy and political manipulation associated with a meeting of the board. All present at this meeting are rich and powerful and all see it as an occasion to consolidate that wealth and power. While the text remarks the presence of the poor in the form of servants, they are typically silent for the duration. And indeed it is the relative silence of the poor that is their hallmark. They are there, but not effectively present. Their voices being usually still, their identity is usually mysterious. Their voices, when heard, come down to us, Annabel Patterson argues, 'by way of ventriloquism, in the texts of the dominant culture'.[2] They are the disguised voices of the bourgeois writer who, Patterson continues, 'must . . . utter, in order to refute them . . . claims whose force may linger beyond his powers of persuasion.'[3] We cannot, that is, trust Shakespeare's representation of the poor as issuing from anything but a condescendingly imagined and represented vision. Indeed, as noted in the previous chapter, familiarity with productions of the plays tends to confirm this notion of their representation, as we accustom ourselves to a condescending lexis which discusses the poor classes, the lower order, the rabblement, and the working people, who are represented usually, though not invariably, as nose-picking halfwits.

The tragedy of *King Lear* involves a struggle for dominance of essentially antithetical economic ideologies. The one, an ethic of individualism, is bolstered and supported by tradition, time, and brute force. It is this ethos which is firmly in place in the beginning and apparently accepted by all onstage. Within this framework,

the poor are essentially instruments of the rich and powerful, and
their welfare is directly dependent on and proportional to that of
their masters. But, it needs to be remembered, the poor are also the
enemy of the rich who control them. The alternative ideology is
what may be and has been called a Christian doctrine of kindness,
charity, and benevolence. It promulgates awareness of and sympathy for the poor whose plight can be ameliorated by a more
charitable distribution of the nation's wealth, but only at the expense of the rich. Given the means by which each of these positions is sustained, it is of course inevitable that the forces of might
and individualism are in the ascendancy.

Cordelia's first words in *King Lear* engage the issue of *having* very
directly:

> Then poor Cordelia!
> And yet not so; since I am sure my love's more
> ponderous than my tongue.

(I, 1, 75–7)

Poverty in *King Lear* is the summons to pity, and yet, Cordelia does
not mean to depict herself here as one of the dispossessed – though
she shall become that shortly, she cannot know it now. Cordelia's
'poor' here means 'unfortunate' – at no point in the play is she
literally poor – except, perhaps, for the brief moment when she
teeters, disinherited and penniless, between her father and one or
no husband. Thus, to extend the logic of this ordinary metaphor,
poverty is bestowed by fortune – birth, accident, luck. By extension,
wealth or fortune derive from the same origins. Thus does one
of the ideas of poverty – its source – serve the culture of wealth.
That is, the rich are not responsible for the poverty of the poor who
have come by their poverty through misfortune or predestination.
Thus, and by extension, any attempt by the rich to alleviate poverty is benevolent and unforced, since the rich are not its cause.
Alleviation will come as a consequence of so-called moral or religious duty, but always as a gratuitous act of good. This is a
convenient reading of the existence of wealth and poverty. It
ignores economic realities that explain the interdependencies of
these two modes of existence – for there to be rich people there
must also and simultaneously be poor people. And yet, surely,
Cordelia's 'poor Cordelia' associates her with the poor in a vivid

verbal manner. If to be poor is to be Cordelia – even only in a metaphorical sense – then to be poor is to share some of her characteristics. For good dramatic reasons, Cordelia is presented as a virtually flawless character. Cordelia's allegiance to virtue and the virtuous characters is adumbrated through the first line she speaks. Her words express her own relation to pity, both pity of the unfortunate and pity of herself, and they are resonantly echoed by Lear's later words, 'I should e'en die with pity / To see another thus.' (IV, 7, 53–4) If poverty is synonymous with goodness, then it is good to be poor – and virtue increases with deprivation in each such case in the play. Certainly the 'poverty' of Cordelia and the later literal poverty of Lear are evidence of their superiority in moral terms to the brokers of power.

Eloquent and pathetic though Cordelia is, real poverty is voiceless in this scene of the play, though it may possibly be present. With the entry of Burgundy and France come '*Attendants*', a silent few who inhabit the periphery of the stage. They remain part of that mainly silent or inarticulate crowd of servants whose being is always subordinate in terms of vocality and physical presence. These attendants, whom I am perhaps presumptuously calling poor, have a number of functions in this scene. Since they are silent but nevertheless there, one of their functions is clearly visual and symbolic. Their presence is normally and reasonably taken for granted by readers and audiences. They are simply appendages to the power politics onstage. But they are vivid reminders of the hierarchical structure of the world of the drama. On the descending scale of power they are at the bottom, a fact reinforced by their silence. Their tacit participation in the scene as attendants – in some productions as map, throne and crown bearers – speaks eloquently of the social order being realized onstage. It is a sign, I think, of the degree to which we are ideologically and historically linked to that social order that we hardly remark these attendants – they are virtually unnoted in reviews and criticism, and it is not expected in production that audiences will pay more than glancing attention to them.

It is worth considering whether they are connected to 'poor Cordelia' or she to them. This long and bitter scene traces the downward travel of Cordelia from her high estate as most favoured princess to her position of fortuneless outcast. She goes from being rich, in other words, to being poor, until she is lifted up by the King of France. What the watching attendants make of this descent is never disclosed. Only the rich – including her sisters, France, and Kent – are seen to react to the distressing event. And yet, as she is stripped of her possessions and land, Cordelia becomes less and less like the members of the court and in fact – even if it is not an obvious one – more and more like the silent attendants. Her refuge in and resort to silence itself strengthens the connection.

But, where the attendants are already in their state of submission and, presumably, want, Cordelia has to endure the process of deprivation, of becoming poor. The tragic potential of the scene and Cordelia's decline are limited by the fact that while she loses her father and her fortune, she is rescued by the King of France. But it is a potential that is played out more fully for King Lear himself. His becoming poor is the nub of the play. Lear reduced from majesty to penury is the story and action that carries the burden of the tragedy and sustains the narrative. His tale imitates that of Cordelia in Scene One, but on an heroic scale. The play is full of reversals of process which turn out sometimes to be advances of truth and knowledge. Lear's recovery of childhood, for example, opens up worlds of emotional and psychological experience that appear to have been uncompleted at the appropriate stages of his life. His reversal of fortune carries with it the burden of psychological, ideological, personal and social history that involves him and his society in wholesale reconsiderations of the entrenched values and political structures.

Impoverishment is a social curse. It means the loss of fortune, friends, and social class. The poor are a constant reminder of the horror of poverty – their plight an object lesson. While the road from poverty to wealth, paved with labour and luck, is the highest social goal and carries the enviable rewards of power and privilege, the opposite trajectory can be a sudden plummet, unwilled and unexpected. Nevertheless, impoverishment is a process, like enrichment. It occurs in space over time. At each moment of the process, the subject's new relationship to the social formation is directly discernible. Tragedy is traditionally and conventionally tied to loss of fortune. And fortune, of course, often refers precisely to wealth. King Lear's fortunes in the play are seen to wane on every level of his existence, but it is surely fair to say that it is through his impoverishment that the play expresses its sense of tragic loss in dramatic and visual terms. Lear's loss of prosperity supplies the image of the extent of his loss of everything else. Poor Lear, who would, at the nadir of his fortunes, die with pity to see another thus, has lost all possessions, all ties to family and friends. His impoverishment seems to him complete; being deprived of everything with social and material value, he is a pauper.

Lear's awareness of his world is not directly or exclusively a consequence of his suffering on the heath in the storm. As his daughters cruelly strip him of his retainers he dredges up from his own memory and experience a knowledge of poverty:

> our basest beggars
> Are in the poorest thing superfluous

> (II, 4, 266–7)

The superlatives of those two lines are noteworthy. They refer to comparisons, to beggars less base and a thing less poor. The fact that overstatement is the normal mode for Lear does not lessen the sense of danger and awareness contained in the words. Lear's future is contained in those lines – ironically or prophetically. He will be the basest of beggars and superfluous in that poorest of things, want.

The crucial 'Poor naked wretches' speech, which draws the world of poverty into Lear's own sphere of existence, is a stage in his impoverishment that offers, for a moment, the fleeting possibility of the softening of monarchical politics. The awareness of beggary is coupled with the recognition that monarchy has abrogated its duty to its poor. However, with the presentation of this crazed and ragged king, the play transcends its own social divisions, offering a view of poverty as experienced from the perspectives of its bourgeois politics. Lear's plight, as he comes to see, is the plight of a multitude of his subjects. It is tragic largely because it is part of the process of disaster, of one who has fallen calamitously to these depths. It is not, as the play might have it, 'natural' to him.

It is, indeed, the ideological form of the concept of nature that the drama explores with such devastating perceptiveness. Lear takes to his new and unforeseeable experience the sensibility and politics of a monarch. He encounters this world of want and depriva-tion with a mind accustomed to knowing it as 'other' and elsewhere. Suddenly he is of this world, and the shock of the realization overwhelms him, as it explains the level and degree and, even, kind of his vastly expanded and altered awareness. He has had to absorb the otherness of poverty to himself, to break down the barrier of otherness as he becomes the thing itself. Here lies the risk of the drama: it wrenches a tired and set old mind from its customary place, and immerses it violently and destructively into that very element that it has evaded. In this way the play is about the nature of knowledge and the relation of knowledge to experience. Lear has always known about the poor naked wretches of his realm. He has, however, never known about them in the way that the play forces him to.

Lear supplies a perspective on poverty that renders its political and social contexts as inextricable, almost symbiotic, links. Poverty is represented as a necessity in the plays and in the wider cultural contexts in which it occurs – including the biblical. *Lear's* world needs poverty because it needs the poor. And, curiously, nowhere does the play question this need. Is not the crucial speech of Lear's illumination simply and directly a statement about the need for charity and the Christian value of benign or charitable feeling?

> Take physic, Pomp;
> Expose thyself to feel what wretches feel,
> That thou mayst shake the superflux to them,
> And show the Heavens more just.

> (III, 4, 33–6)

Shaking the superflux to the poor – which I take to mean giving what is left over – is probably good Christianity, perhaps even good economic policy, but, to risk an anachronism, it is bad socialism. Pomp – says Lear – should not keep what is *superfluous*, but give it 'to them', the wretches who have little or nothing. This done, 'the Heavens' will have been made to seem 'more just', a phrase which anomalously implies less just than merely just. It is a speech, furthermore, which argues that it is the rich – or Pomp – who will determine how the Heavens seem. Justice, in other words, is a human construction within the power and control of the rich. The speech does not, then, stand as a call for justice and equality as some have argued, but rather for an old-fashioned extension of benevolence, kindness, and charity to the poor. But its insistence that the perception of God – the Heavens – will remain the prerogative of entrenched authority reiterates the values of monarchy and hierarchy which have seemed endangered. The rich will retain their dominion over the poor, even in determining the ways in which the poor shall know God. I see nothing in the speech that questions that absolute but absolutely conservative assumption.

The pain and poverty of the pauper/pariah – constructed as the 'other' in Western individualist societies – becomes an obsession for Lear. The individualist politics and poetics that have determined his place in the scheme, and the separateness from others of his existence, are slowly crushed as he is compelled by that very individualism to endure 'otherness' in a wholly new way. It is his individual price, his individualist heroism and sense of worth, that drive him into the storm away from comfort and community. Lear's furious departure from his daughters could happen only in a cultural setting where the self is taught its separateness from the collectivity. His departure, despite its rage and fearlessness, is, nevertheless, a flight from a community that seems to have betrayed its own value of individualism. Rather than meekly submit to his newly and communally defined role as doting father, Lear insists on adhering to his no longer relevant or applicable sense of himself as king. He is, indeed, a sad fool by the standards which he himself has insisted on in his own redefinition of Cordelia. Having passed on his authority with the pomp and ceremony of a religious ritual, Lear finds that he does not like the thing he has done; he has made a mistake. Being now forced to face the consequences of error forces him into new recognitions of his place in the world he had once dominated. Dislocated, disorientated, all that he once knew now seems to have been false. The world was a vast lie – people, places, and things have all betrayed him. He collapses into himself where he discovers his own garden of earthly horrors. Bubbling up from his psyche comes a nightmarish mixture of memories, imaginings, fears, and monsters.

Lear's first sight of living poverty in the course of the drama is in his first sight of Poor Tom. As if by divine intervention, the tragic beggar of his imagination is manifested before him, filthy, alien, naked, incoherent. It is a moment of profound, even catastrophic, shock and it has been well suggested that it is this realization that causes him to lose his wits.[4] And yet, of course, Poor Tom is not the first such beggar Lear has seen. He carries the memory of other such paupers, asking Gloucester at one point, 'Thou hast seen a farmer's dog bark at a beggar?' (IV, 6, 151–2). The basest beggar is a firmly established character in Lear's past. His instant recognition of Tom as having been brought to this pass by 'his daughters' goes beyond mere self-absorbed identification with the beggar. It is a keenly political statement which links poverty with unfair punishment as well as filial ingratitude. That is, Lear's new sensitivity enables him to comprehend poverty as injustice, a notion which flies in the face of the more universal notion of poverty as condign.[5] He is explicit:

> Death traitor! nothing could have subdu'd nature
> To such a lowness but his unkind daughters. . . .
> Judicious punishment![6] 'twas this flesh begot
> Those pelican daughters.

> (III, 4, 70–75)

'Judicious punishment!' is, of course, a sarcasm, at odds with the indignation at Tom's terrible plight.

The entire play circles around ways of having, around abstract and concrete possession. It explores the meaning of possessing things and feelings and also ideological forms like loyalty and love. All such possessings and expressions centre on the individual and his or her capacities for them. Society is represented in *King Lear* as placing a huge burden of responsibility upon each individual for its survival. In this society the primacy of the individual is both its strength and its weakness. Each individual bears responsibility for the wholeness of the whole: that responsibility neglected, the whole is endangered; that responsibility betrayed and violated, the whole can, conceivably, be destroyed. In this representation the play is rather conservative of a moralist notion of order. And, in this light, the play is like a morality drama in the clarity of its valorization of the hierarchy that pronounces order as an ultimate good and its proposition, repeated through the words and actions of characters like Cordelia, that monarchy must be re-installed along lines of 'Christian' wisdom and practice.

But it is within the actions themselves that the stabilizing impulses of wholeness are explored and challenged. The emphasis on having is the emphasis of a rigorous moral and intellectual interrogation of the value of possession. The madmen, beggars, fools, exiles, servants, and blind men of the play make up a large but helpless army of the dispossessed and damaged who are arrayed in scattered opposition to the forces of order. Their innocence of criminality is one thing they have in common, but as a weapon against the heedless military might of the state it is useless. This fact itself challenges the value of order while it does propose an alternative order: the order implied by the image of madmen leading the blind is a symbol of the crazed politics of the Britain of the play, yet the actual mad and blind men, Lear and Gloucester, as images of authority, suggest a reign of innocence and ineffectuality, preferable by far to the megalomaniacal cruelty and vice that in fact governs.

Audiences have tended to understand Lear's tragedy as his fall from prosperity to poverty. His experience of poverty is manifestly unfair and undeserved, and though it teaches him new wisdom, it is a heavy price for him to have to pay for his transgressions. That is the nature of tragedy, of course. The penalty must be out of proportion to the crime. Beggars and the poor are almost never tragic in literature. Indeed, in much of Shakespeare they are, of course, quite the opposite. They are a staple of comedy, whose ludicrousness is usually enhanced onstage by their funny working-class or regional accents and their habits of chewing straw and belching. Poor Tom is tragic and not comic because he is Edgar and, like Lear, is not *naturally* poor. His poverty and madness are his tragedy. But Lear's encounter with poverty provides the galvanic impulse of the tragedy. The act of not having, for the first time, so shocks his system that it almost destroys him. He is appalled to find out that there is a host of paupers out there, in his kingdom, whom he has not sufficiently cared for.

Lear's knowledge of poverty has two forms. There is the old, casual, unfeeling recognition and remembrance of beggars and madmen. And then there is the new recognition of these same hapless beings from the standpoint of shared experience; as a pauper himself, Lear achieves new insights into the nature of poverty. The experience drives the play in unexpected directions. The challenge to Lear's sensibility offered by the new experience of penury must force his audiences to question the same state. As a tragedy, as a dramatic experience that valorizes the individual's plight as the greatest possible suffering, the play encourages the members of the audience and readers to identify 'with' the protagonist in his misfortune. That misfortune is tied to loss – loss of friends, loss of wealth, loss of shelter. The social formation of the first scene establishes these accoutrements of civilization as necessities. An individual who possesses them in abundance or excess is regarded as fortunate; he is powerful and, to use a favourite

Shakespearean word, 'happy'. The concentration of this happiness into few hands is one of the great misfortunes of the worlds of Shakespeare's tragedies for it is always a powerful factor in initiating the tragedy.

It comes to Lear alone of the heroes to perceive this state as a state of national disequilibrium, of political calamity. His perspective, initially turned inward and solely on himself, widens gradually to include the beggars of his world. Peter Brook's *King Lear* is one of only a few productions of the play to have recognized that this particular feature of the disparities in wealth in the kingdom is crucial to the searching maniacal ravings of the hero. In his quest for Cordelia, Lear finds only a dirty beggar and a helpless, bleeding, blind man. Brook's landscape is littered with the embattled and starved victims of the brutality of feudalism. It is Lear's misfortune to have to discover the meaning and feeling of this horror by experiencing it himself. It is surely relevant and interesting to note that in the play the world 'poor' is used forty-one times, more than in any other tragedy; 'beggar' appears seven times. The frequent use of such words lends support to the image of poverty and deprivation that peppers Lear's language and adds to the impression of a beggar-populated underworld in the Britain of this king. These paupers are the 'masterless men' who enter the language by way of Middleton. They speak of a specific danger within the no longer static agricultural society; rogues, vagabonds, beggars, squatters, and the unemployed and criminal poor of London. Lear is alluding to a growing social problem of the dynamic Jacobean era.[7]

Initially, Lear thinks it is possible to divide the kingdom into precisely equal parts. That is, amongst the rich, shared wealth might offer the prospect of peace and contentment. It is a reasoned, logical, politically intelligent choice.[8] The addition of France to Cordelia's third does not imply the inequality of the parts. The division of power and wealth among the three daughters and their husbands indicates a dilution of power, which, in turn, points to the possibility of contention and strife. In this sense the play urges us to acknowledge the high value of unity, of wholeness, of an undivided kingdom. In this manner and in this sphere of its action, the play strongly conforms to and advances an ideology of individualism. But these machinations and calculations occur only on the highest levels of social action. They occur amongst people who are part of the same political and economic interest group. The division itself, however, produces a kind of chthonic truth – that rancour and fragmentedness are more real and normal in this kingdom than harmony and peace. And this is not simply a result of the division, it is clear that this has long or always been so. Goneril and Regan refer to the instability of the king and thus the kingdom as though they were well established facts, and, in so doing, demonstrate the disharmony in action:

> *Regan.* 'Tis the infirmity of his age; yet he hath ever but slenderly known himself.
> *Goneril.* The best and soundest of his time hath been but rash; then must we look from his age to receive not alone the imperfections of long-engraffed conditions, but therewith the unruly waywardness that infirm and choleric years bring with them.
>
> (I, 1, 294–8)

The division of the kingdom exposes and exacerbates the fact of widespread disunity; it does not cause it. By dividing his kingdom Lear has merely let the rapacious brutes out of their cage; the outcome of division was surely inevitable anyway. Britain, we discover, has been held together by the slenderest of threads. In a real sense, the system of monarchy has failed when the mere act of dividing the nation into two parts has been capable of reducing the entire vulnerable, political, economic, and natural structures to rubble. It becomes clear that the nation has been held together by tyranny, but it is curious indeed to observe the growing nostalgia for that tyranny which the displacement of Lear causes. The present spectacle of such nostalgia in much of Eastern Europe is a reminder of the extent to which order on any terms is regarded as preferable to the painful early movements of governments and peoples trying to move away from the tyrannies of the past. Indeed, Lear's famous regretful admission, 'I have ta'en too little care of this', resonates with the recognition of his failure to have united his people harmoniously. That is, it is not merely a recognition of his failure to care for the poor, but an acknowledgement of his rule as suppressive. Any nostalgia for the old days of the old king – and there is very little – is a longing for order at any price, including tyrannical rule.

Lear's tragic journey through the lower depths of his own kingdom in the new role of subject and beggar does nothing to the nation. He has almost literally *become* irrelevant, a piece of the detritus that his monarchy has spewed up – a forgotten, inconsequential man, known or acknowledged by only the hardiest and most loyal of his former subjects. He finds only what has always been there, poverty, rage, and despair in horrible disarray. The erupting nightmares that he gives shape to in his wandering on the heath are an index of the repressive politics of the monarchical regime. Like any beggar he has his passions and hatreds, but, because he is a beggar, these have no external currency. Lear himself, frantic and irrational, is still capable of an ironic wit:

> When I do stare, see how the subject quakes.
> I pardon that man's life. What was thy cause?
> Adultery?
> Thou shalt not die: die for adultery! No:
> The wren goes to't, and the small gilded fly
> Does lecher in my sight.
> Let copulation thrive;

> (IV, 6, 107–13)

The irony, of course, is aimed at himself. A victim of his political rule, he is now a victim of his own king. In this role as subject/victim, Lear experiences beggary *as* a beggar, and not merely as the figment of his memory or imagination. He is one of his own poor subjects. The irony is sharp and trenchant. He has become impotent and worthless. His presence and his threat have become meaningless because he is now one of his subjects instead of himself. Copulation will thrive with or without Lear's permission or encouragement. Lear's cry, 'let copulation thrive!' is a darkly comic permission, a royal command of sexual *laissez-faire*, that draws the tragedy of poverty and want into the realm of the sexual, recognizing the relationship between money, power, and sex that the first scene of the play so vigorously sets in motion. It stands as a farcically violent critique of the doctrine of unfettered individualism that has allowed his own neglect of his own beggars to happen. Indeed, the plight of the king, and his journey through an underworld that he has helped to create, are themselves an implicit attack on the ravages of the politics of individualism.

For behind the pain and suffering endured by so many of the

characters of the play lies the spectre of the individualist enterprise, an ideological formation which, in its desire to serve and
celebrate the dignity of the individual human being, has produced,
inevitably, an economic and political structure which, in the words
of John Stuart Mill, has become 'essentially vicious and anti-social.
It is the principle of individualism, competition, each one for himself
and against the rest. It is grounded on opposition of interests, not
harmony of interests, and under it every one is required to find his
place by a struggle'.[9] That aspect of the individualist agenda was
well underway by the seventeenth century, according to C. B.
Macpherson, who argues that seventeenth-century England was a
'possessive market society',[10] in which individualism had taken
strong hold. *King Lear* is a frightful image of a social formation torn
by the ravages of unrestricted individualism. The cruelty and neglect and the cruelty of neglect – one of the king's greatest crimes –
are referable to the economics of power within the context of a
mania for self-fulfillment and self-expression. Calculated cruelty
like that of Edmund towards his brother is no more or less awful
than the sheer malignancy of Regan who plucks out Gloucester's
eyes for the pleasure, apparently, of causing pain as she disables
an enemy. The monstrosity of the world and the worldly are quite
as appalling as the monstrosity of Lear's imagination; but both owe
their beginnings to the lonely and relentless hunger for self-
definition that is the motive force of individualism.

Notes

1. Dollimore, *Radical Tragedy*, p. 200.
2. Annabel Patterson, *Shakespeare and the Popular Voice*, p. 41.
3. Patterson, p. 42.
4. William Empson, *The Structure of Complex Words* (London: Chatto and Windus, 1952), p. 137.
5. See R. H. Tawney, *Religion and the Rise of Capitalism*, especially pp. 75–89.
6. I take the phrase 'Judicious punishment!' to support my view, and the word 'Judicious' to be flesh-rending and bitterly ironical sarcasm. Most important to me is Lear's perception of his and Tom's plight as punishment.
7. Christopher Hill, *The World Turned Upside Down*, pp. 33–8. Hill sup-plies the source of the phrase; it is Middleton's *The Mayor of Queens-borough*, Act II, scene 3.

8. See Ralph Berry, 'Lear's System', *Shakespeare Quarterly*, 35 (1984), pp. 421–30.
9. J. S. Mill, *Chapters on Socialism* in *Collected Works*, Vol. V, (Toronto: University of Toronto Press, 1963–9), p. 715.
10. C. B. Macpherson, *The Political Theory of Possessive Individualism: Hobbes to Locke* (Oxford: Clarendon Press, 1963).

7

The Politics of Wealth:
Timon of Athens

The obsessive concern of the chief characters of *Timon of Athens* is having and not having money. The question raised by the obsession is not merely what it means to be rich or poor but, more important, how identity is determined by external measurable phenomena like money. The play reveals the extent and the means by which the individual's social locus is fixed and unfixed in relation to such phenomena. Because money buys power and its concomitants like authority, it serves as a convenient signifier of a complex of social practices that has arisen out of the individualist economic framework. There is, as is well known, a rather heavy overlay of morality-play to the drama, a level of allegory that directs attention to a single moral meaning and message about the corruptive power of wealth. *Timon's* world of privilege perceives itself as complete, but one of the inevitable byproducts of privilege and money is poor people: they are slaves, servants, beggars, and whores, and their presence is regarded by the rich without apparent interest. They are not commented on; their plight is unremarked, and they are presented as being without social or political value. Such glaring lacunae deserve attention.

The slow movement from serfdom or villeinage to a capitalist economy, or, as R. H. Tawney describes it, from one nakedly exploitative economic structure to another, is given a somewhat uneasy and reluctant expression in the poor and working people of this play.[1] They are, indeed, humanized, but they are nonetheless located firmly in the margins of the play where their function as a subservient class is primary. For such folk there was little initial difference in the exchange of one form of poverty for another. Feudalism confirmed for the poor the eternal lesson of money's power and its inaccessibility to themselves. But Timon's plummet from wealth to poverty is dramatic precisely because of his former wealth. He has not inherited or deserved his poverty – hence it is the tangible proof of his tragedy. The impecunious Timon is not like any of the other paupers of the play: he is a great man whose sudden poverty seems to have nothing to do with the rational economic context of his world. He is a victim of accident, careless-ness, and the selfishness of the rich. He is a feudal lord in a capitalist economy, and that feudalism manifests itself in his largesse within the ranks of the rich. But capitalism, in the form of greed, complicated evasions, money lending, borrowing, and ex-ploitative relationships, is well comprehended by his fellow pluto-crats for whom friendship is valued in economic not sentimental terms.

The rich, in contrast to the authentically and 'naturally' poor, take for granted that they will not be servants or beggars, but that servants and beggars will always be available for their usage or merely as a means of demonstrating their substantiality to them-selves and others. A remarkable instance of dehumanization and othering – a ratiocinative process of the entrenchment and valida-tion of difference – this process itself sustains capitalism in a primarily Christian world. For the rich to be easy with their wealth, they have to believe that it is their right and their desert that supplies that wealth. To possess it uneasily is an occasional excep-tion given shape in the play by Timon in his last days. The culture of wealth and possession which is certainly the dominant culture in the world of *Timon of Athens,* has woven elaborate justifications of the possession of wealth in a world teeming with the poor and has created practices to sustain it. Religion supplies society with the ideology of charity, whose ulterior purpose, it could be and has been argued (by Karl Marx among others), is to fend off a revolu-tion of the hungry. And economic rationalization focuses on the usefulness of concentrated, centralized wealth in the creation of more wealth and in the relief of poverty. It is probably fair to say that in Shakespeare's plays the possession of wealth is never itself regarded as bad or undesirable, although, clearly, the pursuit of wealth can be profoundly corruptive. In this, Shakespeare is in harmony with most Western economic thought and practice ex-cept, possibly, fundamentalist Christian. There is little in the plays to challenge the moral validity of private wealth *per se* as a good. It is equally true that capitalist thought and practice and its antece-dents have regarded individually-held wealth as a benefit both in itself and in social terms, while socialist thought through the cen-turies has challenged this very concept. The logical corollary to the idea of wealth being a virtue is, of course, that poverty is a vice, and Tawney notes the prevalence through the centuries of the development of capitalist individualism of this way of thinking.

How the rich regard the poor is a constant, if unfocused, theme of *Timon*. The presence of servants and beggars draws attention to their existence, even if it does so only indirectly. They are there; as much, therefore, as the other characters, they may be said to live and breathe and suffer. Their function within this system of having and wanting is to serve. It is left, later, to Timon himself to demonstrate a human condition of absolute poverty, of lacking the very necessities considered basic in human life. He lives uncovered and hungry. Interestingly, a moment occurs in the play when this condition is actually chosen in preference to the condition of having; when the possession of gold is rejected in favour of the possession of nothing.

The moment is rich in irony and ideological contradiction. The discovery of gold coincides with Timon's misanthropic exultation in the bestiality of his fellow men. It evinces a passionate diatribe about the corruptive potentiality of wealth and power. It complements the Lear-like abuse of the world – 'Destruction fang mankind! Earth yield me roots.' (IV, 3, 23) – and inspires the revelation that gold turns morality upside down: it makes

> Black, white; foul, fair; wrong, right;
> Base, noble; old, young; coward, valiant.

> (29–30)

And yet, deep though his loathing is, Timon is himself contaminated by the attraction gold offers – he saves some 'for earnest' (47). The self-exiled, self-outcast crazy recluse is unable completely to separate himself from the corruptive element. He cannot, in other words, escape the taint of wealth because it has become fixed as the agent, symbol, and cornerstone of the society which esteems and disesteems itself according to its relation to wealth. There is no escape to innocence possible for Timon or anyone else in the drama. The whole of the social discourse is tied to the cash nexus. Nothingness, oblivion, freedom even, are inextricable from it. This connectedness of all elements of the system to wealth is visible in the most innocent-seeming moments and the most undefiled relationships. That Timon is related to his 'friends' through his wealth is obvious, even to himself, since he constantly revivifies and nurtures these relationships by money. To his servants too, Timon is implicitly connected by his wealth and their dependency upon that wealth. His being a kinder master than some does nothing to alter the fact that the currency that links them is cash. Apemantus, somewhat anomalously, is a kind of clown, tied to Timon by his cynicism, and wealthy enough to be able to enjoy the luxury of cynicism. Whores and soldiers, like Alcibiades, are themselves dependent upon money for their livelihoods. They, like everyone else in the play, are unable to continue without money.

Money is a gordian knot linking the individual to society. The mad misanthropic violence of the ending, the explosive hatred of Timon for all who come near him, and his helpless desire for the deaths of those around him are merely an expression of the helplessness of penury. And yet, strange though it would be to feel sympathy for the rich men of this play, the problems of wealth are represented graphically enough. Money creates anxiety, and anxiety creates covetousness. The rich man who contemplates the loss of even part of his fortune contemplates simultaneously the weakening of his hold on a social fraction which has taught him that his value is directly equivalent to his fortune. It is clearly anxiety as much as greed that makes the rich unwilling to serve Timon. For their contradictory responses to his newfound poverty indicate a reluctant awareness of their debts to him, a concomitant awareness of his generosity and kindness, coupled with the unwillingness – or emotional inability – to relieve him. They are far from pathetic, and may be presumed to live to a ripe old conscience-free age, but they are surely made anxious by their almost self-aware articulation of the contradiction and the lying to which Timon's poverty forces them:

> Draw nearer, honest Flaminius. Thy lord's a bountiful gentleman: but thou art wise, and thou know'st well enough, although thou com'st to me, that this is no time to lend money, especially upon bare friendship without security. Here's three solidares for thee; good boy, wink at me, and say thou saw'st me not.
>
> (III, 1, 39–44)

Such moments expose greed and dishonesty, and are far indeed from eliciting sympathy for the speaker. Yet they do nevertheless direct attention to the centrality of money as an agent of moral and social change. Furthermore, the greed and dishonesty are represented not as the inevitable expressions of bad characters, but rather as the necessary elements of wealth and power. In other words, this most radical play acknowledges the social sources of corruption and makes no easy correlation between evil and power. The rich are bad because they are rich and not rich because they are bad; this point the drama reiterates time and again.

It is this self-consciousness about the nature of wealth and its relation to society that makes the play less transformative in its impulses than *Lear*, to which it is often compared. It is this same quality of self-consciousness that makes it a more intellectual and controlled dialectic about the social and individual meaning of wealth and its implications for the collectivities in which Timon lives and is forced to live. Before he is poor, Timon never needs to question the meaning of having money. He is a rather flamboyant philanthropist, doing good deeds by ostentation, chiefly in behalf of those who seem not greatly to need his largesse. Once his money has been lost, its meaning, its presence as a dynamic factor in his life, suddenly become matters of bitter urgency to him. We have his two worlds sharply and evenly divided.

While the poor of Athens are neither enriched nor further impoverished by the fortunes of Timon, the rich are found depending upon him to sustain their positions of wealth. Nothing that occurs in Timon's wealthy phase, in other words, suggests the rich protagonist's awareness of the poor. Once he is poor, however, it seems to him as though all the poverty in the world is his, all the wrongs done by rich to poor are wrongs done to him. In this concentrated and narrow awareness, he is the opposite of Lear who perceives in his penuriousness that he has taken too little care of the poor, that he and they share crucial human matters. Timon is so consumed with the rage for revenge against his humiliators that other people become less and less important. As Lear is reabsorbed into the world he once controlled from the heights, so Timon is alienated from his world by his poverty. The poor are the dirty little secret of both worlds, but far more passionately acknowledged by Lear than by Timon. Yet their sheer presence as a quiet force is a factor in both plays where they represent the potential plight of the powerful.

Timon's poverty is represented as unique, as wholly separated from that of his fellows. He has nothing in common with the whores and servants with whom he is forced to keep company. In this separation lies much of the secret power of the play and much also of its complex politics. In *Timon of Athens* it is not power but poverty that corrupts. The ancient notion of poverty as a sin, as an evidence of moral worthlessness, is given a kind of extensive play in the variegations of narrative and the pungent invective of the drama. As ingratitude drives Timon into frenzies of rage against his former friends, so poverty takes him further into the catastrophes wrought by revulsion. As Lear sees poverty with the eyes of pity and shame, so Timon sees poverty as a grotesque deformation of his desert. The point is crucial. The informing power of loathing is given expression in filth and rage and self-pity. The view of poverty as a punishment and wealth as a reward had, by Shakespeare's time, replaced the view that poverty and material inequality were socially necessary.[2] Thus, the justice for which Timon clamours sits firmly within the individualistic politics of the play.

The notion of their own poverty rolls easily off the lips of the rich, but only when it is notional. Before the warm-water banquet, the Second Lord tells Timon, 'I am e'en sick of shame, that when your lordship this other day sent to me I was so unfortunate a beggar.' (III, 6, 40–2) And it is this casual, crass, linguistic, and wholly insincere familiarity with poverty and beggary that the narrative seeks to expose as one of the many disguises by which wealth distances itself from poverty. It neutralizes the lexis by which poverty is constructed and so makes it harmless and unthreatening. To be poor does not mean as it does in, say, *Lear*, to be penurious and lacking in necessities. In the mouth of the Second Lord and his like, to be poor means to have less money and comfort than one would like or than one thinks one deserves. It means to be less rich, perhaps, than one's friends, who seem to supply the standard of measurement. Thus it may be suggested that wealth corrupts language itself from a motive of the nakedest self-interest. For poverty is a potential threat to Timon and his fellow millionaires. Through reconstructing it linguistically, they effectively stave it off, make it part of another world than the one they inhabit. Beggars are others than themselves, yet they appropriate beggary by absorbing it into their language and experience thereby, in effect, distancing it further from their own real experience. As a metaphor the word loses its ties to the fact of actually not having and comes to suggest something far more harmless. When not having a great deal of ready money can be described as being in a state of beggary – as above – then beggars are not taken seriously. In a similar fashion it is common to hear comfortable or uncomfortable middle-class people describe themselves as being poor. The description inevitably denotes a devaluation of poverty, robbing it of its conceptual power and value.

One of the evidences of wealth is the possession of servants. All the rich, notwithstanding protestations of poverty, always have servants. Yet poverty and beggary are constantly on their tongues. The play is populated with characters from the poorer classes. Servants, prostitutes, robbers, a page and a clown. Though, indeed, as Rolf Soellner notes, poverty 'provides no total immunity from the [temptations of fortune].'[3] Commenting on the servants, Soellner notes 'how sympathetically they are portrayed. One cannot attribute their benevolence merely to their choric function or underline the pathos of Timon's fall. . . . There is no breakdown in servant morality of the kind that Malynes and other critics found in England and that Timon proclaims in his craze for total upheaval. . . . Yet, one cannot take much satisfaction in this goodness from below. Its most salient feature, after all, is its impotence, and it seems susceptible to perversion too.'[4]

The conclusion of the warm-water feast provides an example of the means by which wealth insulates and protects itself from the reality of penury. The lords, having been driven violently away by Timon, conclude that he has surely gone crazy:

> Second Lord. Lord Timon's mad.
> Third Lord. I feel't upon my bones.
> Fourth Lord. One day he gives us diamonds, next day
>   stones.

> (III, 6, 113–15)

The reverse side of this collective reprehension is, of course, a kind of cheering up of themselves as blameless victims of Timon's irrational rage. The lords separate themselves from their former patron and friend by agreeing to absolve themselves and blame Timon. But it is the word 'mad' that gives them release from their responsibilities to feel and act upon guilt. Timon has been put beyond the pale and reach of help by his own 'madness'. His madness, they conclude, is a 'natural' product of his own self-induced poverty.

The play exposes the hoax of the natural in a remarkable way. Shakespeare seems to have recognized two vital points: one is that the ideologies of his culture are political and partial, that they are determined and defined by those with the power to determine and define ideological formations – that is, the ruling class. Secondly, that the vaunted ideology of naturalness is anything but natural; rather, it is formed out of the desire and need to control society. Thus, the 'natural' bonds of parent and child, or husband and wife, or ruler and subject, or brother and sister, need the sustaining support of institutionalized systems and structures of law to be enforced. Pascal noted that 'Fathers fear that the natural love of their children can be erased. What kind of nature is this, that can thus be erased? Custom is a second nature that destroys the first. But what is nature? Why isn't custom natural? I am very much afraid that this nature is only a first custom, as custom is a second nature.'[5]

The naturalization of wealth as the prerogative of the wealthy is one of the essential functions of the rich in the play. They believe that they deserve their wealth, they possess it 'naturally'. To allow things to seem otherwise is to permit the idea of the opposite – that they do not deserve or have a natural title to it. A consequence of such thinking is, of course, for them to have to surrender that natural right. Wealth and possessions and their concomitants, power and security, fit comfortably into the doctrines of individualism. As a complex of values, they neatly submit to the motive forces that drive individualism and are malleable enough for their achievement to be valued more highly than individual doctrines that might hamper it. In *Timon of Athens* the behaviour of Timon's friends, after he has lost his fortune, must surely throw into question the means by which their wealth was won in the first place. Besides wealth itself, in other words, what has wealth brought them? The answer is plain: anxiety, cupidity, dishonesty, greed, cruelty, crookedness, hypocrisy, selfishness, cowardliness. It is true that all may have possessed these traits before they became rich, but it is wealth that has made them matter socially, that has given credibility and political force to their lies.

Where *King Lear* throws the entire value system of individualism or, in its seventeenth-century form, possessive mercantilism,[6] into question in its recognitions of the social injustice deriving from *laissez faire* economics, so too *Timon of Athens* interrogates the economic and political roots of greed and crookedness. Like Northumberland, in 2 *Henry IV*, who calls upon mankind to destroy itself because he himself has been injured, Timon's hurt elicits from him a desire to hurt others, all others, innocent and guilty alike, because of what he perceives them to have done to him. His betrayers are not merely, in other words, his treacherous friends, but all the inhabitants of the city.

His massive curse outside the walls of Athens reconstructs the entire Athenian society in its hierarchichal order. In pouring his venom on the society he lays bare its structures and hierarchical arrangements of power. Notwithstanding the wild, ranging ubiquitousness of his hatred, Timon retains a clear sense of the order of the world he has left behind him. His attack on Athens is an attack on the political ideologies which give it its identity; these are related directly to its power nexus, itself an integral part of its cash economy. The first target of Timon's wrath is, tellingly, female chastity, which is arguably the cornerstone of patriarchal individualist economic structures. When he cries, 'Matrons turn incontinent' (IV, 1, 3) and, a few lines later, 'To general filths / Convert, o'th'instant, green virginity!' (6–7) he is striking at the very heart of that thing by which individualism, patriarchy, paternalism, and, above all, primogeniture are maintained. Take but chastity away and the entire system by which poverty and wealth are determined falls to pieces. More sinister by far than Lear's misogynistic outpourings near Dover, Timon's assault on this most vulnerable and uncertain means of sustaining patriarchy derives from a driving impulse to bring about social collapse. The world of *King Lear* has a Cordelia and a Kent in it, memories of whom draw Lear away from total nihilism. *Timon* is a play remarkably without heroes or heroism; it provides Athens with nothing worth saving from the blight of Timon's bitter curses.

It is intriguing indeed that Timon, like Lear a man who has stood at the top of his society, should recognize in retrospect the force of sexual control as a chief means of maintaining social order. The release from sexually responsible behaviour, brought about by their outcast states, reveals the extent of psychological and social repression that has been necessary for social order to reach the form and extent it has. The concentration of Lear and Timon on female sexuality, and the form that their feelings about women take, reveal two crucial constructions of gender and sexual relations: first of all, it is evident that both men regard women as their *natural* enemies; as people who would take up arms against them if given the means. Secondly, it would seem that the gynophobia of

Timon and Lear derives from a series of beliefs and assumptions about the inherent propensity of women to unrestrained sexuality. In his catalogue of reversals, Timon attributes power to women in only one area – that of sexual behaviour. An unsurprising concomitant of this sexuality is the implication that sexuality is equivalent to vice.

Where Northumberland's invocation of the 'spirit of Cain' calls forth, even from his supporters, a cry of shame, Timon's cry of hatred for Athens possesses no such corrective. As Athens has been exposed, and has exposed itself, as corrupt and evil, there is no evident reason to save it. Its treatment of Alcibiades and Timon are evidences of its failure. Thus, in his raving, Timon produces an abstract of the ideologies and institutions which hold the society together:

> Piety and fear,
> Religion to the gods, peace, justice, truth,
> Domestic awe, night-rest and neighbourhood,
> Instruction, manners, mysteries, and trades,
> Degrees, observances, customs and laws,
> Decline to your confounding contraries;
> And yet confusion live!

> (IV, 1, 15–21)

This delineation of the social and civil categories with a view only to their destruction marks this scarifying speech as utterly and unrelievedly subversive to the point of complete upheaval. A. D. Nuttall proposes that in this speech, 'fierce contrariety of mind reaches out towards and almost touches the practical contrariety of social revolution.'[7] The basis of social revolution, however, is always regeneration, which is surely the last thing on Timon's mind here or ever again. The frantic curses of the speech possess and are possessed by an overwhelming desire for the apocalypse.

All elements of the curse conspire to one end; that of the reign of poverty and one of its frequent Shakespearean synonyms, criminality. *That* is the nature and extent of Timon's apocalypse. It is to this that his curses point. When he calls on Destruction to 'fang mankind' (IV, 3, 23), he is placing himself far from redemption and into the centre of a maelstrom of death and destruction. For, indeed, there is unchastity and promiscuity in the play in the form of the prostitutes who visit Timon in his cave. And it is their example that this diatribe anticipates and summons down upon Athens as a dreadful curse. The speech adumbrates a world in which order is upended, not destroyed. This is the nature of the vengeful curse. Timon's revenge will be, if the curse is realized, not an absence of order such as that summoned by Lear and Northumberland, but an inversion of it, so that his former friends will now themselves be ruled by their former servants and outcasts:

> Bankrupts, hold fast;
> Rather than render back, out with your knives,
> And cut your trusters' throats! Bound servants steal!
> Large-handed robbers your grave masters are,
> And pill by law.

> (IV, 1, 8–12)

The notion, of course, transcends any idea of social revolution, upholding, as it does, the value and practice of criminality. There is no question of the replacement of vice – the rich – with virtue – their servants. No sense, in other words, of providing the disenfranchised with a voice or an opportunity. Nuttall quite reasonably points out that the servants of the play whose 'hearts wear Timon's livery [still]' (IV, 2, 17) are 'pathologically loyal.'[8] And Ralph Berry, in discussing the exemplariness of the servants, reminds us that the Steward 'seeks out Timon in the woods, to serve him still. Even Timon admits him "one honest man". So the relationship of master and man, which might seem to be founded on money, escapes the play's nihilism.'[9]

Prostitution supplies the most resonant metaphorical means for the destructive impulses of the drama. It is, of course, one of the abiding evidences of the frailty and duality of patriarchy. The ubiquitous and universal condemnation of prostitution has done nothing to slow its pace. The male use of women takes no more tangible or obvious form. Timon treats the prostitutes loutishly. Though he is an outcast, and though they are outcasts, he regards them with withering contempt; they are corrupt and tainted. He treats them like dogs whose silence he can purchase. The scene in which they and Alcibiades visit him in the woods ends up restating the power of money to divide humans into classes. Timon's misogynist abuse of the prostitutes takes his earlier gynophobia several steps further. Prostitutes are the lowest class of people in the play and the worst treated. As though men had nothing to do with them or their profession, the prostitutes are reviled by Timon as diseased creatures unworthy of human communion beyond their ability to contaminate and sicken men and help to fulfill his project of destroying Athens. In the whores Timon finds the metaphor he seeks for the filthy condition of humanity and the instrument he seeks for destroying it:

> Hold up, you sluts,
> Your aprons mountant. You are not oathable,
> Although I know you'll swear, terribly swear
> Into strong shudders and to heavenly agues
> Th'immortal gods that hear you. Spare your oaths:
> I'll trust to your conditions. Be whores still;
> And he whose pious breath seeks to convert you,
> Be strong in whore, allure him, burn him up;
> Let your close fire predominate his smoke

(IV, 3, 136–44)

And yet, when Timon was at the height of his powers, he was little different from this. Though benignly, he did entertain his guests lavishly with Amazons, unthinkingly, smoothly, as a mark of his silky generosity. The distinction between the prostitutes and the 'Ladies as Amazons' is purely contextual. All 'belong' to men, all are defined and dehumanized by their functions; the Amazons to caress men, the whores to burn them up with disease. A potent loathing is expressed by the curious but resonant phrase, 'Be strong in whore' which, oddly, has the effect of encouraging while it condemns, thus setting Timon above the corruption he is so eager to employ. Their function is their belonging, their capacity to be possessed and purchased like goods by money. And then, hypocrisy of hypocrisies, Timon, who has purchased women himself to entertain his guests, who has taught dependent women their obligation to cash, damns the whores for accepting the gold he throws at them.

Though Timon is, in some measure, unthoughtful, quick to conclude but slow to examine, there is no reason we must follow his suit. Each evidence of want in his world he transforms into a means to blame and destroy the 'Athens' that has injured him. His rages against Apemantus as he stalks the woods are the passions of

a towering sulk. Apemantus sees neediness, he acknowledges the
inequity and cruelty of the 'Athens' of the rich. He taunts Timon to

> Call the creatures
> Whose naked natures live in all the spite
> Of wreakful heaven, whose bare unhoused trunks,
> To the conflicting elements expos'd,
> Answer mere nature; bid them flatter thee.

> (IV, 3, 229–33)

Such recognitions in King Lear are praiseworthy. Why not so in
Apemantus? He sees the vanity and pride of Timon, though not,
perhaps, the perverse depths of his fury: 'Thou'dst courtier be
again / Wert thou not beggar.' (243–4)

Outside the walls of the city, Timon is imprisoned by a violent
shame born of shock, disappointment, outrage, and helplessness.
The injustice to himself is different from that to other men because
he was born to his wealth, had – in other words, or so it seems –
earned it by inheritance, a curious but common notion.[10] That it
has been taken from him is a greater injustice than if it had been
taken from someone else who had earned it by sufferance and
labour. This is surely a most odd economics, but one which Timon
is resolute in. He rages at Apementus:

> But myself –
> Who had the world as my confectionary,
> The mouths, the tongues, the eyes and hearts of men
> At duty, more than I could frame employment . . .
> – I to bear this,
> That never knew but better, is some burthen.

> (261–9)

And then, self-righteously:

> Thy nature did commence in sufferance, time
> Hath made thee hard in't. Why shouldst thou hate men?
> They never flatter'd thee.

> (271–3)

Timon, outcast, poor and dirty, still insists on his rights and privileges as a rich man. The distinctions would be comical if he were not so passionately serious about them. Because the world was his confectionary his right to hate it is as great as his right to possess and direct it had been. No others need apply. The mastery of Timon is indisputable and the economic and class system which produced in the society the means of ingratitude and the divisive propensities of an economy of wealth and poverty must remain intact or be completely destroyed.

His passion is his blind hatred for all. Timon never loses his naive idealism, clinging furiously and hopelessly to the patriarchal model which is so contingent on the wealth of individuals. He transforms the citizens of Athens in his mind into thieves as vicious and culpable as the Banditti who seek his gold. They are all alike in their betrayal of the morality of money. They all steal it, Timon insists, and thus have not the right to it that he had:

> To Athens go;
> Break open shops: nothing can you steal
> But thieves do lose it.

> (IV, 3, 449–51)

It is his exemption of himself from the general curse that robs his rage of moral fervour and makes it look like colossal spite. Timon is a Malvolio who has lost the will to live. His hatred is purer than Malvolio's because it includes himself. There is no thought in him of survival or social victory within Athens. Whereas Malvolio, right to the end, seeks to triumph over the society that has humiliated and betrayed him, Timon rejoices in his separation from it. He luxuriates in his perception of Athens as not worth conquering, unless it be to destroy it utterly, not worth living in or being part of unless its values have been inverted and deformed. It has been said often enough that Malvolio is a tragic figure in a comic play. Timon is a Malvolio writ large, a tragic figure of rage and violence in a tragic play, unembarrassed by the consolations of the slapstick which doesn't really hurt. Timon plummets to death by way of wrath.

His splenetic rages and universal curses are a volatile mixture which explodes in destructive frenzy. Timon's is a tragedy of disorder and chaos. No healing precedes or follows his death. The conditions of greed and covetousness that produced the conditions that drove the hero from his home are still firmly in place. Knowing this, Timon is merciless. He invokes the agents of chaos; he calls for the violent deaths of his countrymen by any and all means. Timon's last spoken words amply fulfill his lust for the suffering of his fellow Athenians. His invitation to them to hang themselves on his tree tauntingly expresses his loathing. Between his last speech and his two epitaphs is a curious continuity of action. He speaks his words of venom to the senators while his steward's benignant presence here disturbs the validity of the tirade. With 'Sun, hide thy beams, Timon hath done his reign' (V, 1, 221) the last spoken words of Timon are given voice, and he disappears from sight, curiously lingering on in memory through the bitter self-dramatizing epitaphs. These have the effect of grandly excommunicating the whole insanely materialist world, reducing it to inconsequence and worthlessness.

The analysis of wealth which constitutes the play has exposed the revolutionary nature of this tragedy. No sense of loss accompanies the declining fortunes or the death of the hero. Values have been robbed of meaning, death is a release even for a robustly aggressive character like Timon. There is no purpose left in his life once disillusionment has taken hold of his imagination. Betrayal, weakness, and dishonesty are what are left of the ruling class of Athens. Its painters and poets collaborate cheerfully with its ruling faction in the frenetic pursuit of wealth. Those citizens on its margins, its mad hermits, its servants, its whores, haunt the periphery of the once proud city, waiting for it to fall to the military machine of Alcibiades, himself yet another victim of its distorted mercenary values.

Notes

1. R. H. Tawney, *Religion and the Rise of Capitalism*, p. 69.
2. Ibid., p. 36.
3. Rolf Soellner, *Timon of Athens: Shakespeare's Pessimistic Tragedy* (Columbus: Ohio State University Press, 1979), p. 121.
4. Ibid, p. 120.
5. Quoted by Stephen Greenblatt, *Learning to Curse: Essays in Early Modern Culture*, p. 94.
6. C. B. Macpherson, *The Political Theory of Possessive Individualism, Hobbes to Locke*.

7. A. D. Nuttall, *Timon of Athens* (Boston: Twayne, 1989) p. 87.
8. Ibid. p. 87.
9. Ralph Berry, *Shakespeare and Social Class* (Atlantic Highlands, NJ: Humanities Press, 1988), p. 163.
10. The question of inheritance as a prop by which elites are formed and class differentiation sustained is addressed in the next chapter.

Part III

8

Measure for Measure and Liberalism

The streets of Vienna are odoriferous. They carry the stench of crime and licence. They exude a knowingness that reeks of excess and decadence. The denizens of the streets have all been there a long time. They talk with nasty familiarity of sexual illness and rape. One of their number is sentenced to death and they joke about it, supplying a kind of Hell's Angels' sympathy for a comrade who has gone down fighting the good fight. Lurking beneath the surface of this jaded world is a potential for violence and destruction that has been kept in check by a liberal ruler who understands full well the capacity for absorption and appropriation which his leniency possesses. Permission and permissiveness have bred soft dissatisfaction in the city, while they have allowed it to increase without apparent danger to the state. The streets are inhabited by madams, pimps, johns, and whores who live on the edge of the law, aware of its elasticity and essentially free to flout it at will.

In his liberality, disguised as kind-heartedness, the Duke of Vienna has discovered a means for containing violence and political dissatisfaction. Though sexuality seems to be the obsessive metaphor for freedom in the play, in fact it is a systematized liberalism[1] that ultimately forms the political control of the leadership of Vienna. If the hallmark of liberalism is, as Terence Ball and Richard Dagger argue, the attempt to promote individual liberty,[2] and if individualism has always been a central tenet of liberalism, as is recognized by all writers on the subject of liberalism, it would seem that the position of the Duke of Vienna, and the play itself as a political expression, are explorations and critiques of some of the essential dilemmas that the liberal agenda has always implied. These include, almost above all, questions of freedom and liberty and the question of the relation of the individual to the group, and the relation of the individual to capital. Liberals, for example, agree, and critics of liberalism confirm, that a basic tenet

107

of the ideology is the belief that self-interest is the primary motive
for most behaviour. The characters of *Measure for Measure*, almost
without exception, are seen to act from motives of self-interest.
They assert themselves individualistically in such a way as to
demonstrate their own freedom from the collectivity.

Most citizens seem to have been content under Duke Vincentio's
easy rule. Normalcy has been redefined; sexual freedom seems to
have usurped the place of political dissent. Those who have been
critical of this regime are silenced by, on the one hand, cooptation
into the echelons of power – Angelo – and, on the other, by the
biological-political imperatives of sex–gender – Isabella. But for the
majority living is easy and dirty. A casual world without work or
responsibilities is the way of things.

The state, however, has grown fat under this regime of leniency
and satiety. Permission has bred satisfaction and excess. There is
no rigour or backbone left, or, rather, what is left has become so
deformed in reaction to the permissiveness that it is as dangerous
to the welfare of the state as leniency has been. We know what
could have happened had Angelo been indeed given the power
that the Duke promised him and which he thought he possessed.
Angelo is ready in the wings with an orgy of punishments for
transgressors of his personal code of righteousness. We can imagine Isabella as governor: she too believes in the rule of the
righteous and supplies the fearful possibility of imposing that on
the rather innocent citizenry of Vienna. Angelo's dissatisfaction
with the politics of Vienna is personal and religious, as is Isabella's.
Their own codes of decent behaviour and moral propriety are
violated with impunity by their fellow citizens. The state, according to Vincentio, Angelo and Isabella, needs a firm hand to restore
its moralistic toughness. Fortunately for the ever-lucky duke, the
citizens are leaderless. Cynicism prevails, and the easy attitude of
immediately accessible self-gratification subsumes discontent and
dissent – until Angelo. The street people of this play are not
noticeably poor or disadvantaged, there is no complaining about
the lack of money or necessaries. There is, on the contrary, a
noticeable air of sufficiency. And, indeed, Angelo's crime, in the
eyes of the 'Viennese', is that he threatens that very sufficiency.
Angelo's Puritanism almost anomalously signifies the dangerous
presence of that threat to luxury. The anomaly, of course, lies in
the fact that, as R. H. Tawney maintained, Puritan ways of
thought, while condemning ease and excess, contributed signifi-

cantly to the development of a capitalist outlook:[3] money yes, but morality also – a contradiction in terms to some.

There is an ordinary middle-class Vienna, a Vienna of business and family and normal bourgeois life, but it is almost invisible in the play. *Measure for Measure* includes in its characters and actions chiefly the outrageous and the aberrant. Somewhere out there, on the margins of the unfolding drama, are citizens who are carrying on in the predictable way. The whorehouses in the suburbs, for example, are not, after all, to 'stand for seed', but have been purchased by a 'wise burgher', presumably as a good financial investment. The burgher is unnamed, unknown, invisible, but he stands for that world of everydayness which is so egregiously absent in the play. One may be reminded of places like Lebanon during the worst years of the civil war. We, the consumers of massively produced news, were prevailed on to forget that in Lebanon, despite the ravages and horrors of the wars, life went on for most people. They went to the beach, they did laundry, they carried on business, they had children and, even, outside the zones of killing, peacefully buried their dead. Shakespeare's Vienna is presented in like manner: it is a place burgeoning with conflict and vice and corruption and violence. It is only in the shadows that we find more and other than the drama expresses.

That 'wise burgher', in other words – and the adjective carries an interesting freight of moral and political implications – is rather more interesting and important than we might care to think. He emphatically is not part of the corruption and violence or, even the moral callisthenics of the chief business of the play. But he supplies instead a quiet standard and reminder of normalcy beyond the narrow confines of the action. His wisdom, accepted as a given, consists in his opportunistic self-interest. The play, in other words, is rooted and contextualised in a surround of petit-bourgeois business and opportunism that too easily becomes over-shadowed by the high drama of the death plot and its ramifications for all concerned. The concept of the alienation of property – the ability to buy and sell it – is regarded as central to the doctrine of liberalism which, though its roots extend farther back and deeper than the sixteenth century, did not become systematized until a good deal later than that. Nevertheless, as C. B. Macpherson reminds us, 'Liberalism had always meant freeing the individual from the outdated restraints of old established institutions',[4] and clearly the wise burgher of this drama is participating in a system of liberal capitalist endeavour made possible by the embryonic liberal capitalism of the late sixteenth century. And Macpherson is almost alone among the socialist theorists of liberalism in arguing that liberalism is not an inevitable and integral component of capitalism.[5]

The wise burgher is not the end of the bourgeois life in Vienna. Anthony Arblaster states that the 'metaphysical and ontological core of liberalism is individualism'[6] and demonstrates, further, the rootedness of liberalism in an 'isolation of each human being from his/her fellows'.[7] The individualism underlying the political assumptions of *Measure for Measure* is the very ideology that produces the sense of each character as existing in a solitude. The walls that stand between characters in their most yearning moments are a sign and a recognition of the loss that is sustained when individualism dominates the polity. It needs to be recognized that this way of thinking was a departure from the medieval notion of the individual as incorporated within society, and that the individualist and liberal notion dramatically challenged the idea of the isolated striving individual as being radically incomplete or inadequate.

Although, inevitably, the play deals with the questions of motive and morality, it is equally and concomitantly an arena for the struggle for dominance of ways of life and modes of rule. Each of the modes is, significantly and revealingly, consistent with liberal practice. Each mode, those of the duke, Angelo, and Isabella, is both produced by and, anomalously, promises the continuation of the ideology of liberalism – a liberalism perhaps naively and incompletely formulated, but liberalism nonetheless. The unacknowledged marriage proposal of Vincentio to Isabella – proposals would be more like it – is a strong indicator not only of the patriarchal structure at its most flagrant and overbearing, but also of the isolatedness of the two self-involved and rather sadly lonesome figures. Their individual plights at this conclusive juncture in the play come from their separately tragic assertions of self at the expense of and in isolation from the community. Angelo's equally tragic isolation – seen especially as he becomes aware of his stunted sexuality – is not because he has spent too much time in the library, as common lore has it, but because he too is a subject and, even, a victim, of the ubiquitous thrust of individualistic endeavour. The bringing together of the isolated individuals of the drama under the most arbitrary of circumstances at the end of the play is an index of the futility of the attempt to do so. We are left, at the end of *Measure for Measure*, with a set of marriages whose participants have little in common beyond the fact of a relation to the world and worldly goods that bodes ill for the futures of all involved. Their arrival at that moment of failed commonality has been, in a sense, predictable from the outset. All three – and the 'others' to whom they are arbitrarily joined – have been in pursuit of self-expression under a kind of aegis or permission of the prevailing ideology of individual isolation and 'liberal' politics.

The marriages of Vincentio and Isabella, Angelo and Mariana, Lucio and his 'punk' indeed perform the conventional function of ensuring the continuation of the social formation under traditional comedic conditions. That is, the serious side of marriage is taken care of by the generally unhappy coupling; the carnivalesque, celebratory side of marriage, however, is gloomily absent. Marriage is represented in each of the cases listed, as well as that of Claudio and Juliet, as an obligation or duty or, even, punishment. These austere manifestations make a mockery of the notion of marriage as an affective relationship between people which had become current at the time of the play.[8] But far more urgent than the marriage question posited by the conclusion is the question of resolution that the facts of these marriages raises. The question is observable on several levels relevant to the discussion of liberalism.

Essential to the promotion of the liberal agenda is the stability of the middle class. The implications of this statement have a strong bearing, of course, on the question of money and goods and their relation to the polity. Capitalism, it has been argued, is one of the crucial concomitants of liberalism, as class is one of the central components of capitalism. A class, which can be and has been loosely defined as rich and poor, or rich and middle and poor, is more exactly, in the words of Macpherson, 'those who stand in the same relations of ownership or non-ownership of productive land and/or capital.'[9] As in most 'citizen' plays of the period, *Measure for Measure* concentrates closely around the middle class, with only the occasional venture into the peripheries of poverty or riches. Its characters are not absorbed by the question of money; it is there and it is taken for granted.

Liberal ideology has always strongly supported the right of inheritance; in doing so it has helped to define and perpetuate an elite class and thus confirmed its status as a roundly class-based political ideology.[10] And it is indeed curious to see how the issue of inheritance affects matrimony and love in almost all of the relationships awaiting resolution in the drama. The centrality of private property to the liberal doctrine and to the action of *Measure for Measure* accounts directly for the misery of at least half of the marriage partners of the play's conclusion. The saddest case of all is Isabella's. She who sought to renounce wealth, property, and marriage is dragged back into the world of money, materiality, and sex without a thought as to her desires, but with a tacit notion that the acquisition of wealth through an alliance with the duke – 'What's mine is yours, what is yours is mine' (V, 1, 534) – will be sufficient to obtain her compliance with the idea of marriage. The cliché itself rings loudly in our ears as a phony commencement to an incompatible coupling. That incompatibility is elaborated by the multiple marriages of the conclusion which, as a set, make a mockery of the touted reconciliation and reintegration of the social formation which are sometimes thought to be among the glories of comedy. The sense of division is stronger at the end of *Measure for Measure* than it was in the beginning very largely because the reconciliations of the conclusion have been subjugated to the overarching reach of patriarchal individualism.

Isabella's attempt to achieve self-expression by entering a convent is an example of one of the few ways in which it may have been possible for a woman to separate herself – only partially – from the male order of the world. Granted a male-dominated church, within the sisterhood a woman would have found sisters – other women – and would, as Isabella clearly is, be immediately answerable to a woman superior. The submission to a male church and a male God would have been more abstract in the life of the nun in the convent than in the outside world. Isabella's silent acceptance of her new role as wife to the duke – *his* duchess, after all – stands as a jarring indicator of the impossibility of female escape or independence. The rather brutal triumph of patriarchy and liberal individualism is proclaimed by her silence and the duke's conquest. That silence is resonant with protest and suggestive of unease. Isabella knows with a knowledge born of hard recent experience that the equation of 'mine is yours and yours is mine' is only the merest tokenism and pretence of equality. The liberal individualism of the world she inhabits is liberal only towards men of property and encourages only their individuality. She knows, as her recent encounters with Lucio, Angelo, Vincentio, and Claudio have demonstrated, that it is her inescapable lot to be a subject of men, a man, and the male world. It is perhaps to speculate too far, but not, I think, too fancifully, that Isabella has come, at last, to the recognition that the church she once venerated has betrayed her in almost the same way that the men of Vienna have. In its many male forms of a sanctioned but false friar, real but manipulating and oppressive friars, and its agents, nuns like Sister Francisca, the church is her enemy; it commands her submission.

Isabella's defeat is the cruel tragedy of her life; her gender is her destiny and her submission is predictable and inevitable. For a man, however, this is not how even primitive liberalism is supposed to work. It is, on the contrary, supposed to give hope and freedom to him, to sustain his individualism and validate his self searching. It is Angelo who is most utterly betrayed by the individualist political dogma. He tumbles into some of the fearful traps of individualism. He takes to a logical extreme the freedom he is given. He finds himself caught in some of the contradictions of individual freedom and religious restraint. And the play takes a fascinating detour through the thickets of community to the islands of self as through the political history of the late renaissance. The play perceives and represents religion and the constantly visible Church as political entities, as sources of government and restraint. The power of the Church in seventeenth-century political life can scarcely be exaggerated. Christopher Hill writes of the huge extent to which the parson and his superiors, the landed ruling class, influenced the political, economic, and moral outlook of the populace of the early seventeenth century.[11] The Puritan ideology supplied precisely such a trap to the ambitious man. It encouraged notions of community while it simultaneously validated and promoted individuality. 'Puritanism', writes Hill, 'supplied a superb fighting morale. It appealed to men with social consciences, to those who felt that the times were out of joint . . . and that they could and therefore must help to set them right.'[12] A logical extension of such politics is authoritarianism, or the conviction that one's superior knowledge or morality may and must be imposed on others – for their own good or the good of the community. The question of Angelo's own fall is problematic within the limits of this aspect of Puritanism. It is a question he himself asks: does his own weakness and incapacity to live up to his ideals invalidate those ideals? Is there not a socially constructed system which can and must support those ideals for the sake of the common good? In the light of the complexity and inherent

contradictoriness of the agenda Angelo is pursuing, it is not ad-
equate to argue that mere individual hypocrisy can undermine the
political system that is in place.

Angelo's tragedy is great because the forces of self, so tightly
reined until the meeting with Isabella, break loose and plunge him
into a vortex of conflict and confusion which transform his every
hope and fear. His life is uprooted, his beliefs are shattered, his
world is turned upside down, and the system in which he has
staked his life and faith offers him nothing in the way of comfort or
support. He must go on to his death. He acknowledges this fact
while he heroically, even if perversely, persists in the path into
which he has strayed. His soliloquies after the fateful encounter
with Isabella are filled with fear, and rage, and intimations of
death. He is in every sense, except the theatrical, a doomed man.
Living, as it were, takes on a life of its own for Angelo. Hating
himself, hating what he is doing, Angelo carries on, taking himself
to the brink, impelled by forces he loathes utterly but understands
fully. His speeches are replete with awareness of the contradictions
of his plight, contradictions which foreground the conflicting
interests of the liberalized individual and the social formation:

> What's this? What's this? Is this her fault or mine?
> The tempter, or the tempted, who sins most, ha?
> Not she; nor doth she tempt; but it is I
> That, lying by the violet in the sun,
> Do as the carrion does, not as the flower,
> Corrupt with virtuous season. Can it be
> That modesty may more betray our sense
> Than woman's lightness? Having waste ground
> enough,
> Shall we desire to raze the sanctuary
> And pitch our evils there? O fie, fie, fie!
> What dost thou, or what art thou, Angelo?
> Dost thou desire her foully for those things
> That make her good?

> (II, 2, 163–75)

The striking discursive movement of this passage is its compulsive
renegotiations of the speaker's personae. From a first person
singular voice, Angelo repositions himself in relation to his subject

into a first person plural stance, and then, finally, into a third person singular stance, so that from being himself and acknowledging his own locus in relation to his criminal intention, he ends up addressing himself as 'Angelo' as though the original 'I' had become distanced from the subject and the would-be victim. The question is, then, who is addressing the 'Angelo' of the passage? Who is asking, 'What dost thou, or what art thou, Angelo?' That very capacity to anatomize the self into many selves, to reidentify and relocate the selves, is a byproduct of a world conditioning itself more and more to an individualist agenda.

Angelo's confusion of identities can be related to the separation from the collective that is the essence of liberal individualism. The self as a connected unit, as a part of the whole, becomes destabilized as it is divorced from the integrated community whose interest is represented as inimical to the individual. Of course, liberalism includes and supplies hedges which protect the community from the ravages of individualism, but it does so hortatively and persuasively through laws and codes. What it cannot do is to resolve its inherent contradiction. Thus, in crisis, the human subject is confronted with those contradictions and their hopelessness of resolution. Angelo attempts to resolve his crisis through comprehension, through speech, in effect. His questions in the speech allude to doubt and disturbance, to the fact that all of the certainties by which his political credo has sustained him until now have crumbled.

Angelo's career directs attention to some of the dangers of the liberal ideology. If, as has been argued by the leading philosophers of liberalism, ideology and individualistic capitalism are inextricably bound, then it must follow that liberalism is a profoundly and irrecoverably elitist philosophy.[13] Clearly not all individualists can achieve power, and yet the entire ideology stands upon the acquisition and use of power and, as it gets closer to the twentieth century, to the myth of the equality of the accessibility of power for all. However, in reality, the power and possession of some must equal the disempowerment and dispossession of others. The example given above of the entrenchment of inheritance well underlines the point about the creation and stabilization of an elite class. *Measure for Measure* can be read as one facet of the crisis of individualism. It is, perhaps, not going too far to say that Shakespeare's plays collectively and individually are obsessed with the contradictions and confusions which are innate to the philosophic formations that, in combination, gave rise to capitalism. Capitalism cannot exist without liberalism and individualism; the anxiety of the plays and the crises of their individual characters are almost directly referable to the conflicts of freedom and restraint indicated by the rapidly increasing separation of the individual from his moorings in community. Claudio's words, early in the play, ring ominously with the sheer irreconcilability of the introrsed pressure from the contending ideologies:

> *Lucio.* Why how now Claudio, Whence comes this restraint?
> *Claudio.* From too much liberty, my Lucio. Liberty,
>   As surfeit, is the father of much fast;
>   So every scope by the immoderate use
>   Turns to restraint.

> (I, 2, 116–20)

Claudio's reply belongs entirely to the ethic of individualism. He is, in essence, arguing for moderation on the grounds that excess or extremism turn against themselves. He speaks as though it were a law of nature, as though nothing were more obvious; and wouldn't it be nice if it were true? However, what is really implied in Claudio's rule is a wish-thought of liberalism; that is, that the practice and its philosophy contain within themselves the means of its own regulation. Yet, this idea of natural self-regulation is, in a philosophical sense, the very antithesis of the individualist agenda which has tended to justify itself by arguing the existence of such restraints. In a sense, then, Angelo, for all his authoritarian impulses, is by far the more honest and self-aware ruler of the play notwithstanding his use of menace and lies. The logical means towards the regulation of an uncontrolled state is not, as the duke proposes, moral pressure and self-imposed moderation, but, indeed, tyrannical oppression and the ruthless application of the laws. A compelling political check on individualism, which, as Hobbes was so eloquently to argue, resulted from the inevitable subordination of reason to desire, was the regulation of desire by legislation and authority.[14]

It is, however, Duke Vincentio who is testing the outer limits of an individualist and liberal political system. In what is surely one of the most appallingly self-serving speeches known, he freely admits that he is using an unwitting Angelo as his *gauleiter* to

restore public respect for the law by the latter's predictably excessive adherence to its letter. His position is simple: Angelo is a
known martinet whose enforcement of the law will be so strict and
unpleasant and punishing that his subjects will gratefully welcome
back the duke who, by contrast to Angelo, will seem an angel of
mercy in their eyes.

> I have on Angelo impos'd the office;
> Who may in th'ambush of my name strike home,
> And yet my nature never in the fight
> To do in slander.

> (I, 3, 40–3)

The law, and the authority to wield it, is not the index of power.
Power, real power, is the ability to comprehend and extend its
limits. The duke knows this truth with a machiavellian clarity that
makes Angelo look like a babe in the woods – which to some extent
he is, albeit a mighty dangerous one. This use of Angelo is, as a
host of contemporary critics have noted, as cynical a project as one
could imagine. And yet, all this use and abuse of power occurs
within the confines of a dukedom which has many of the birthmarks of a liberal democracy. For although the ultimate political
and judicial authority of this state is one man – Vincentio – the
impulses of individualism are given wide scope in the experiment
conducted on a merely surrogate ruler who takes the bit in his
teeth and, as it were, runs with it. Angelo is an experimental
subject. His individualistic propensity is being cynically tested
with the object of determining how far it will be taken. His desire,
as Hobbes would have easily predicted, subsumes his reason,
while his instinct for self-preservation remains firmly intact. But
that is, in large measure, what individualism always is understood
to be, even by so benign a later apologist for liberalism as John
Stuart Mill.[15] Liberalism implies the belief that most people are
capable of living freely, that they have the ability, through reason,
to control and direct their desires.[16] Angelo, the arch-rationalist by
reputation, the passionless man, is the instrument by which the
duke tries the proposition. The final production of a pseudo-
Hobbesian truth against a more liberal-minded one is utterly sub-
verted by the play's unavoidable retrospective acknowledgement
of the Duke as a liar.

Though it is always Angelo who is accused of abusing power, it is surely Vincentio who is the more culpable ruler. His abuse consists of the exploitative use of Angelo. The duke is, simply, a liar from the beginning of the play, a liar who later admits that he has known about, and has had an interest in, Mariana and Angelo's treatment of her. He has known, in other words, about Angelo's crooked unreliability from the beginning. By contrast to this kind of disingenuous scheming, Angelo's frantic urge to stamp out sexual promiscuity seems merely simpleminded or naive, and the excruciating things that happen to him cruelly unnecessary. Certainly, the crazed, vicious plot he weaves against Isabella gives him more unhappiness than it gives her, both immediately and ultimately.

One of the more interesting ways in which this play explores the liberal-capitalist ideology is in the very clear distinction between the ways the different classes regard and feel about sex. The history of the criticism of the play demonstrates the extent to which the critics have aligned themselves with the upper class or the court. There, amongst the rich, sex is a complex social and psychological matter hedged with stringent prohibitions. Above all, sex is forbidden outside wedlock. Though, of course, this is hardly an invention of the capitalist ideologues, it was, nevertheless, a feature of earlier economic and political ideologies that fit the capitalist agenda like a glove and was not abandoned by western culture until well into the late twentieth century. It has always been the case that sexual behaviour has been a greater source of anxiety within the propertied classes than among the working and poor classes. Criticism has been fairly united in condemning the street people of the play for their far more ('too') casual attitude to sex; they seem to regard it as a merely natural activity, like eating and drinking. They construct it in natural and animal terms, and don't, in general, seem to take it terribly seriously. For them it is an easy fact of life. This attitude has made them odious to most critics of the play who thereby align themselves with the play's forces of decency and authority.

Angelo and Isabella have an equal horror of the sexual. The power of sexual feeling has less to do with appetite than with the way in which it has been socially constructed by religious and economic pressures as a secret, forbidden, private, and somewhat degraded function. These pressures have come, historically, from those authorities in whose interest it has been to control and regulate sexual behaviour. Hence, those classes with property and, therefore, power have had more pressure to regulate their sexual behaviour than those in which fewer social and political consequences follow from sex. Both Angelo and Isabella, scions of the middle and upper classes, exemplify some of the horrible effects of the practice, within their pasts, to regulate and deal with sex by the quasi-liberal and individualist societies in which they live or have lived. The story of Angelo's repudiation of Mariana for the reputation of sexual laxity and/or loss of her dowry is a fitting exemplum of the relation of property to sexuality.

Indeed, the real noisomeness of the streets of Vienna is not in the casual attitude to sex but in the permeating notion of prostitution as a 'normal' and 'ordinary' sexual activity as though it were somehow removed from the political and ideological. The street folk of the play are mightily culpable in this one regard: they regard prostitution as natural in the way that sex is natural, ignoring the economic and political relation of prostitution to the state and its means of survival. Angelo's desire to raze the brothels and put an end to prostitution is a radical subversion of one of the chief safeguards of social security and tranquillity tolerated by the lenient but wily duke. Prostitution, as the remarks on the subject by such as Lucio and the Gentlemen strongly indicate, is one of the duke's means of stabilizing potential disturbance; it is part of the 'sport' (III, 2, 116) that is sex for the street people of the drama.[17]

The liberal polity possesses an elasticity that is sufficient to absorb and appropriate dissent and upheaval: it can contain limited dissent or subversion without feeling threatened.[18] By extending the political agenda in one direction – that is by permissiveness in sexual matters – Vincentio deflects potential politically disruptive energy in another. Given the duke's rather ready willingness to use such women as Mariana and Isabella to achieve his goals, it is hardly surprising that he would find the use and tolerance of prostitution an amenable political tool. Prostitution is an appropriate symbol of his reign in which human beings are used as though they were mere commodities or goods; the tolerance of prostitution in a society where women are disadvantaged says nothing favourable about the liberality of the ruler who is prepared to show a blind eye to the practice which is, after all, in this play, merely a matter of men's usage and convenience.

The relation between freedom and property, and hence liberalism and property, is a question which is central to the development of liberalism. Citing several sixteenth- and seventeenth-century English writers on the subject, Arblaster gives a picture of a society in which wealth and property are privileged and fixed as indices of power and social standing.[19] Self-interest, one of the bedrocks of the entire liberal philosophy, is represented as plain common sense by Thomas Wilson in 1572: 'What man is so madde to deliver his moneye out of his owne possession for naughte? or whoe is he that will not make of his owne the best he can?'[20] With the precise relation between wealth and political power being identified, it followed that a large majority of non-property holders were entirely without political power. These included the poor and virtually the entire female sex. The latter category takes a somewhat deviant form in the play. Mistress Overdone is clearly a property-owner and entrepreneur. She owns the prostitutes and the brothels, and her lament when she hears that they are to be pulled down – 'What shall become of me?'(I, 2, 97) – places her squarely in the ambit of the free traders and propertied gentlemen of the drama. In a world of excess and deviancy, the capitalist-madam is merely another anomaly in a market economy; this has always been the case with female brothel-keepers.

Angelo's faith in the system in which he lives and labours is nowhere more tellingly and, even, touchingly stated than in his description of his ruler as 'power divine'(V, 1, 367). Lucio, whose punishment, for reasons never understood by me, is even harsher than Angelo's, presumably feels less the victim of divinity and more the victim of sneakiness and bad luck. Angelo's confession is also the last words he speaks in the play:

> O my dread lord,
> I should be guiltier than my guiltiness,
> To think I can be undiscernible,
> When I perceive your Grace, like power divine,
> Hath looked upon my passes. Then, good prince,
> No longer session hold upon my shame,
> But let my trial be mine own confession.
> Immediate sentence, then, and sequent death
> Is all the grace I beg.

(364–72)

The success of liberalism has rested always upon the belief in an hierarchical allocation of power. This speech, guilt-laden as it is, locates the source of power in the duke, recognizes his almost divine authority. There is an uncomfortable aura in Angelo's recognition and the duke's cooperation in it, of the idea of the 'supreme leader', a notion which is certainly at odds with the liberal enterprise, although very compatible with the dogmas of individualism. There is surely an unintended but biting irony in Angelo's characterization of the duke as a kind of holy authority when his entire project has been to effect a secular miracle by deception and disguise. And yet, Angelo's words are a clear surrender to the forces of reaction and the doctrine of conservatism as he repudiates his own revolutionary and individualist endeavour. Angelo's melancholy acknowledgement of his own weakness and the duke's power is a kind of recognition of the failure of his attempt to act individualistically and independently. In *his* eyes, the conservative forces not only have triumphed over the radical alternatives that he has provided, but, also, they are associated in his mind with the forces of right and morality. Shakespeare, more subversively, has indicated the limitations of this simple view of things by offering a duke who is hugely compromised in terms of the very things Angelo submits his life to – his exercise of power and his moral probity.

In *Measure for Measure* the street life plays a remarkably active role in the drama as a whole. It is not, as in other plays, clearly separated from the other echelons of activity. Rather it permeates these echelons at all levels. It brings us a powerful, mostly disguised, ruler into shoulder-rubbing touch with the lowest prisoner and the most characteristic street person. The lines of separation, so vividly marked in, say, the histories, are blurred in the action of this play, though retained less visibly in the separation of verse and prose. There is an illusion of democratization occurring in the drama. The disguised duke is taken for an ordinary friar, and outwardly he behaves like one. His easy manner with the various people with whom he is in contact makes the idea of his absolute authority over them somewhat questionable. If he can equal them, why cannot they equal him? The question of power and authority over people's lives is, of course, paramount to a discussion of liberalism. This play supplies an image of an essentially feudal government which is radically interrupted time and again and in a multiplicity of ways by the intruding reality of liberal individualism. Duke Vincentio has lost his austere dignity, that mysteriousness that makes him an unquestioned and absolute ruler. The concluding dialogue is redolent with this loss. The duke engages in an absurd argument with Lucio about the punishment he has ordered. Lucio almost mockingly resists and rejects the idea, protesting that it is too harsh. The duke's final retort to Lucio is a rather desperate attempt to restore some of his lost standing:

> *Lucio.* Marrying a punk, my lord, is pressing to death
>   Whipping, and hanging.
> *Duke.* Slandering a prince deserves it.

(V, 1, 520–2)

Vincentio's penultimate enforcement of his authority – I take his proposal to Isabella to be the last such – is to chastise and punish a slanderer. So much for ducal grandiosity and the quasi-feudal authority that this duke has attempted to recover. So much for what Edmund Burke was to call the 'true natural aristocrat', he who possesses the ability, the experience, and the inclination to govern wisely in the interests of the whole society.[21] Overall, there is an air of confusion that hangs over this play. In it certainties are challenged, conformities are deformed, expectations are thwarted, and philosophies are deracinated.

Notes

1. Though the word 'liberal' did not enter the political vocabulary until the nineteenth century, the ideology and practice of a primitive liberalism commenced in the late medieval period. Indeed, J. Salwyn Schapiro argues that the roots of Liberalism can be found in Socrates and Peter Abelard. See *Liberalism, Its Meaning and History* (New York: D. Van Nostrand, 1957), pp. 14 and 94–7.
2. Terence Ball and Richard Dagger, *Political Ideologies and the Democratic Ideal* (New York: Harper Collins, 1991), p. 49.
3. R. H. Tawney, *Religion and the Rise of Capitalism.*
4. C. B. Macpherson, *The Life and Times of Liberal Democracy* (Oxford: Oxford University Press, 1977), p. 21.
5. See *The Life and Times of Liberal Democracy*, pp. 93–114.
6. Anthony Arblaster, *The Rise and Decline of Western Liberalism* (Oxford: Basil Blackwell, 1984), p. 15.
7. Arblaster, p. 21.
8. See Catherine Belsey, *The Subject of Tragedy: Identity and Difference in Renaissance Drama* (London: Methuen, 1985), pp. 149–91.
9. Macpherson, *The Life and Times of Liberal Democracy*, p. 11.

10. Arblaster writes, 'It will, however, be generally accepted that the ability to transmit wealth and advantage from one generation to the next is at least one of the means by which a perhaps temporary elite converts itself into an entrenched class.' p. 90.
11. Christopher Hill, *The Century of Revolution: 1603–1714* (Aylesbury: Nelson, 1972), p. 77.
12. Hill, p. 82.
13. Macpherson is one notable and famous exception; though in recent times, especially since the collapse of the Soviet Union, this position has become more popular amongst political theorists. See *The Life and Times of Liberal Democracy* where he argues the compatibility of liberalism and socialism.
14. Arblaster, pp. 132–5. 'Hobbes . . . once again undercuts later liberal optimism, which interpreted the "blank sheet" or *tabula rasa* theory of the mind as the basis for a faith in the transforming potential of education, by pointing out that those whose minds are like "clean paper" are also "fit to receive whatsoever by Publique Authority shall be imprinted in them"' (p. 135).
15. Macpherson writes that though Mill believed that people were capable of becoming something other than self-interested acquirers of benefit to themselves, most of them had not got beyond that. *The Life and Times of Liberal Democracy*, p. 56.
16. Ball and Dagger, p. 51.
17. Zola's description of sex as 'the poor man's opera' in *Germinal* is an interesting complement to such remarks, suggesting, as it does, that the political reality of sex is different for rich than for poor.
18. Modern liberal states, like almost all industrialized Western nations, have easily been able to accommodate communist parties within their capitalist economies. This flexibility is, of course, only possible while the oppositional ideologies do not actually threaten the stability and superordinacy of the dominant liberal ideology. Once that threat exists liberalism breaks down.
19. Arblaster, pp. 150–2.
20. *A Discourse upon Usury*, quoted by Arblaster, p. 150.
21. See Ball and Dagger on Conservatism, pp. 91–117. I accept the fairly respectable and widespread assumption amongst theorists of liberalism; that conservatism, as it was and as we know it today, is a branch of liberalism.

9

The Madding of Malvolio

One of the many disturbing facts about mad people is that they do not fit into the usual social, political or economic categories of class, race or gender. Their social *loci* are thus difficult to determine, and their relation to the social nexus remains unfixed and uncertain. Indeed, though they unavoidably belong to one or more of these groups, they also transcend them all by belonging to that more marginal group of the insane where normal categories get lost. Shakespeare's madfolk are kings (Lear), queens (Lady Macbeth), princes (Hamlet), rich commoners (Timon), young innocent women (Ophelia), and beggars (if Edgar is not an actually mad beggar, he does an imitation of one that convinces even the savviest characters in the play). These characters have in common their madness, a condition which has a unique source in each case and always takes different forms: it issues from rage, disappointment, guilt, fear, frustration, or shame. Like Caliban himself, the mad person is a true outcast from society, one who has the special capacity to induce both awe and disgust. It is the uniqueness of madness, the fact that the mad are mad alone, isolated and separated from their fellows, that makes them both frightening and harmless. Though there have been instances of mad people discovering common cause, it is seldom that they act in unison. The tragedy of madness is, perhaps above everything else, its loneliness.

Madness is like a terrible disabling deformity. It situates an unwilling subject in an adverse and opposite relationship to the social formation. The mad person dwells in a world that is mysterious to the group: he or she can utter the most incontrovertible human truth, but the utterance will be regarded as tainted by the madness and hence expendable. Thus, Polonius's famous remark about the method in Hamlet's madness is also and simultaneously a way of denigrating the method as issuing from a disabled imagination. The method is thus seen as accidental and may be ignored because it comes from a contaminated source. The examples abound. In a discussion of madness as a form of political

124

radicalism, Christopher Hill confirms that 'Many radicals recognized . . . that their views were so extreme that they must appear mad to normal members of the ruling class.'[1] And he notes the possibility that political radicals of the period may at times have adopted the disguise of madness in order to 'express dangerous thoughts under cover of insanity or delusions, from which [they] could retreat afterwards.'[2] The normal mad person, however, is the individual whose behaviour is determinably bizarre and inappropriate and usually results in him or her being shunned or marginalized. If they are sufficiently mad – read physically or intellectually dangerous to other people – mad people are locked up with other mad people so that society may be safe from them or their ideas.[3] So that, as soon as they are transformed into a group or collectivity, they are subjected to the violent suppression of confinement which makes them harmless to the community which their madness disrupts. Hill writes about the sixteenth-century practice of using mad people as entertainment.[4] Though that is no longer acceptable practice, it is not easily demonstrable that our entertainments today have become more refined or less cruel.

The mad person is threatening because he is seen by the world to have reordered or renegotiated his relationship between his self and others; he seems to lack the desire or ability to distinguish between the private (inner) self and the public (social) self. This makes him unpredictable: a remark or perception can be produced from either realm with reference to either realm. Such unpredictability can disrupt social discourse and the normal flow of social intercourse. The potential danger to society that results from the fusion of interior and exterior selves is socially acknowledged in the universal practice of separating mad people from society. It is ironic, but significant, that the only mad person in Shakespeare to be involuntarily separated from and confined by society – that is, the only character to be treated like a mad person – is one who is not actually mad, Malvolio. The treatment of Malvolio, not only by his tormentors, but also by those who have been convinced of his madness, gives strange insights into this form of marginalization and, in general, to this process of determining and treating madness, which is itself also a form of social self-preservation.

The mystery and the sacredness of madness are of a piece with its horror. This is its puzzle; its irrecoverable ambiguousness. In searching for the perplexing source of this ambiguity, Enid Welsford asks the searching, unanswerable question: 'Who then is this

Fool? Is he . . . a descendant of the old sacrificial victim, and if so, why is he regarded as a Fool? Was he once the village idiot, chosen for slaughter because his lunacy rendered him at once sacred to the gods and useless to the human community . . ?'[5] The way in which mad people can be regarded as wise seers is part of the mystery. Their truths discomfort because they lack the restraints that obtain in ordinary, normal life. Thus the madness becomes a permission to speak with the kind of unrepressed freedom that is denied the rest of us. There is, thus, a power in madness which complements the contradictory debility that it also implies. R. D. Laing has written eloquently about the political implications of madness, about the arbitrary construction and definition of madness and how it is used as a political tool, and about how culturally determined a construct it can be. He makes the point that the social system in which the mad person lives may be 'insane' or inhospitable to the person it conveniently labels insane: 'the experience and behaviour that gets labeled schizophrenic is a special strategy that a person invents in order to live in an unlivable situation'.[6] Madness can be and often is used by the dominant authority or culture as a means of political suppression (the modern Soviet Union provided one notable example amongst many through the ages). Laing urges,

> It is not enough to destroy one's own and other people's experience. One must overlay this devastation by a false consciousness inured . . . to its own falsity. Exploitation must not be seen as such. It must be seen as benevolence. Persecution preferably should not need to be invalidated as the figment of a paranoid imagination; it should be experienced as kindness.[7]

Since one of the central tenets of any definition of madness is unconformist behaviour, obviously political non-conformity can become identified with madness. As this, clearly, is the case cited by Christopher Hill, so too this, surely, is Malvolio's case.

Even the most conservative critics have sensed the political threat that Malvolio stands for in relation to his social 'betters' – including Sir Toby and Sir Andrew, but also including Lady Olivia and the Duke himself. His relation to them is one of class resentment; he reasonably perceives himself as a more valuable member of society than they: he at least works and makes a living. His arduousness in his profession of steward is something of a living reproach to the accident of birth that dictates that he shall work and they shall dally. His desire to enter their class is the instilled desire of most disadvantaged people in the world to share in the world's riches that are normally enjoyed only by the privileged. There is a symbiosis between the powerful and the powerless that relates them with unbreakable bonds. The powerful have that which they have taught the powerless to desire – the powerful hold the reins of value and culture and determine that which has and has not value in society. The powerful can only have what they have because the powerless do not have it.

Malvolio, in a manner of speaking, is mad long before he is declared mad – normalcy in this Illyrian world is a perversion of the normal. He is regarded as a kind of sociopath and disliked by the ruling class to whom he has a limited access because of his servant status. He stands for order and an ethic of work, austerity, and abstemiousness in an ambiance that seems to value everything but such practice. That he harbours secret desires that contradict what others understand to be his way of life is not a proof of hypocrisy. He wants what he believes he deserves but what his lowly station forbids him even to *want*.

It is an interesting and unsurprising fact that Malvolio has long been regarded as the embodiment of right-wing politics by the Shakespearean critical tradition. It is interesting because that tradition has been deeply mired in a form of liberalism which has become virtually indistinguishable from right-wing conservatism itself. According to a number of political theorists such as Anthony Arblaster, liberalism and conservatism have less to distinguish themselves from each other than their proponents would wish.[8] Both ideologies are firmly rooted in the same pre- or early capitalist ideologies and both are inseparable from expressions of individualism. This lack of a real or major distinction is nowhere so demonstrable as in literary studies of the last two centuries. The identification of Malvolio as a Puritan reactionary is largely a means of putting a somewhat illusory distance between a 'liberal' politics which regards itself as humane, decent, and democratic and a 'right-wing' or 'conservative' politics which it (the liberal critical tradition) regards as autocratic, selfish, and decidedly undemocratic or authoritarian. It is unsurprising that Malvolio has been stigmatized with reactionism because his personal and political traits and ambitions usefully and egregiously fulfill the liberal idea of reaction. He has a lust for power and for using power to control and manipulate others autocratically – but it is, after all, a secret lust to which we become privy by decidedly unfair means. His fantasy marriage to Olivia (Act II, scene 5) has him wallowing in bed as he gives orders to his erstwhile master, Sir Toby Belch. I daresay that this exactly is the power and the fatal attractiveness of wealth, and that this is the occasional dream of all servants – that is, of imaginatively putting themselves in the position of wealth and authority just because it is the very antithesis of what their relative poverty and servitude force them to endure. Malvolio's Puritanism is represented and then demonstrated as a form of gross hypocrisy which secretly conceals a sybaritic sensualist. Shakespearean drama, of course, has no respect for privacy and uses it as a primary means of betraying characters and making public what is assumed to be utterly private. Thus, the inner conflicts of Malvolio are fodder for comedy and self-exposure *because* he is spied on by others who wish to destroy him. And thus too, the inner life and fantasy of Malvolio, and any other dramatic character for that matter, are given a significance and relevance to events in the material outer world which they could not possibly possess in reality. It goes without saying, however, that in daily life all people are happy *not* to be judged by their private thoughts.

I suppose it is an exaggeration to say that Malvolio is mad anyway. But there is a determinable social pathology in the environment he inhabits that is far worse for him than it is for, say, Viola or Sebastian. Malvolio starts out as the recognizable enemy of virtually everyone he meets, with the exception of Olivia. To others he is a drag, a clog, an impediment to the fluidity and ordinary rituals of life. To the wastrels and the Fool, his authority in Olivia's household makes him a threat to their freedom and irresponsibility. That threat has potentially serious consequences in Malvolio's wicked and unforgiveable denigration of Feste's professional ability. His job is one which demands that he be or become an unloved servant of a spoiled, self-indulgent mistress. It is his responsibility to curb the excessively joyous noisiness of the wastrels. The play's famous line about cakes and ale is unfairly used against Malvolio if we can, for a moment, take seriously the position of economic and political dependency in which his fortunes and birth have placed him.

The punishment of Malvolio is carefully designed to entirely disable him. It is simple: his tormenters plan to render him impotent by making him the object of universal ridicule by allowing him to act in such a way as to seem mad. Their best weapon is their faith in his own overweening vanity. The vanity is the curious and volatile element in this mixture. Malvolio commits the cardinal error of believing that he is worthy of the romantic favour of a woman who is his employer – who stands above him in the social and economic scales. His aspiration towards such a woman is read as a kind of madness which argues a gross lack of self and social awareness. It would appear that the laws of nature are being challenged by Malvolio's crazed ambition – except, that is, for one thing:

> There is example for't. The Lady of the Strachy married the yeoman of the wardrobe.
>
> (II, 5, 36–7)

The quiet insertion of a precedent, a known fact, into a seemingly wild fantasy introduces an element of reality and possibility into what is insistently perceived as a ludicrous and crazy notion. Such things, in other words, *are* thinkable. Malvolio's radicalism lies in his belief that he is good enough to be married to Olivia. His self-valuation includes the possibility that he could marry above his station into the aristocracy of what is, after all, Illyria, where the improbable is normal. The Lady of the Strachy and her yeoman of the wardrobe are submerged by the raging farce and soon forgotten. Malvolio has demonstrated his upstartness to the two audiences who are spying and watching, and thus, on one level, he has proven his detractors to be right about him. He deserves punishment for his overweening ambition, and no more fitting punishment is conceivable than to take from him the self-validating pleasure of being heeded.

Proving Malvolio mad is an easy matter. He is, to start with, vain and individualistic enough to believe in himself as a potential suitor to his rich, beautiful, and aristocratic mistress. That reason and memory have helped him to this pass does not make him seem less mad: he recognizes how his mistress values his service and, of course, the Lady of the Strachy married her own yeoman of the wardrobe. He reasonably believes that his mistress has declared her love to him in only somewhat ambiguous terms. All of this, however, is grist to his enemies' mill: to Olivia, the sight of Malvolio making love to her with looks and words and gestures is sufficiently strange behaviour to help warrant incarceration. His

form of courtship of Olivia is an indication of his pathological
naïveté. He is tricked into using every device of courtship calculated to alienate the object of his affections. In word, gesture, and
appearance, Malvolio gets everything horribly upside down. His
doing so derives from an erroneous belief that the class system is
more elastic and flexible than it is. If, indeed, Malvolio is a Puritan,
then his faith itself will have validated his sense of the artificiality
of the class boundaries which seem so fixed to the other characters
of the play. Christopher Hill has noted the democratic implications
of Puritanism,[9] implications which would, surely, have given a
Malvolio the audacity to consider the possibility of marriage to his
mistress.

His tormentors know that Malvolio is not mad and Malvolio
knows he is not mad. Yet his treatment as a lunatic has a plethora
of implications and manifestations designed to sustain the notion
of his madness. First of all, there is the isolation of the subject. He
is separated from his fellow humans, confined, imprisoned, out of
harm's way. Alexander Leggatt's suggestion that the lone, tragic
voice of Malvolio crying in the dark is a kind of audial symbol of
the isolatedness of the characters is a trenchant insight into the side
of sadness and separateness that is so insistently, if subter-
raneanly, present in the play.[10] The person who has once been
incarcerated as a lunatic, instantaneously brings down on him or
her self the terrible curse of Cassandra. The more he protests his
sanity, the less he is believed. For someone in a madhouse to claim
to be sane is only to confirm their madness and to validate the
authority that has put them there.

The act of singling out and scapegoating Malvolio has intriguing
social and political roots. The marginalization of one character for
such a purpose has a close likeness to a characteristic tragic action
where a crisis is resolved through the pursuit, discovery, and
destruction of a character who can be said to embody the rage and
the illness of the society. René Girard observes that if a community
in crisis is to be freed of responsibility for its unhappy condition,
the violence and distress of the community must be deflected to
some individual.[11] 'How does it happen', Girard asks, 'that the
community's sense of unity, destroyed by . . . crisis, is suddenly,
almost miraculously, restored? Here we are in the very midst of the
crisis, when all the circumstances seem to militate against any
unified course of action. It is impossible to find two men who agree
on anything . . . No connecting thread, however tenuous, links

the conflicts, antagonisms, and obsessions that beset each individual.'[12] Malvolio becomes the means by which the diverse and distinct classes of characters are united. Their concentration on him, first in his madness and then in their simultaneous exposure and recognition of the joke he has become, is a crucial element in creating the sense of unity and harmony of the play's conclusion. While they do not in any real sense kill their scapegoat, the other characters set him outside the pale of the society and unite in their recognition of his outsideness.

It is possible for all groups within the society to use Malvolio as the kind of scapegoat whose demise heals social ills only because of the way madness functions. Because Malvolio is 'mad', his relation to social class loses relevance. As a mad member of society he becomes both the scapegoat and the responsibility of the group. They must care for him and protect themselves from him. His incarceration causes a concentration of sympathetic and antipathetic energy on him. Once he is declared mad, Malvolio is rendered harmless to all. Those whom he sought to injure with his authority and ambition are safe from his malice and bullying. It is interesting to note the imbalance or disproportion of the feelings of the wastrels and Malvolio for each other. Malvolio's fantasy gives him away. He longs to call Sir Toby, 'Toby' or 'Cousin Toby', and to order him to 'amend' his drunkenness. (II, 5) He wishes to patronize and condescend to him. Sir Toby, by contrast, wants to attack Malvolio violently and to injure him physically – 'O for a stone-bow to hit him in the eye!'(II, 5, 42) – to cudgel him(122). The concentrated rage which Malvolio arouses in Sir Toby has as much to do with the knight as it does with the steward. The aimlessness of life in Illyria for all but the servants produces manifestations of boredom and unease in the duke's subjects, as in the duke himself. The shifting points of focus in love, in grief, in pleasure argue a kind of endemic restlessness that is almost at a crisis point and that calls for the cleansing purgation of wrath. Consequence has lost consequence, direction and purpose dissolve. Sir Toby's violent rage is not only his fear that Malvolio threatens his way of life, as a whole generation of critics suggested, but also that through Malvolio and his very palpable ambition, Sir Toby can find an objective externalized source of his own debility. The desire violently to destroy Malvolio is an expression of the desire to address and rid himself of that debility as though it were, in fact, something outside of himself. The only inhabitants of this luckless place who have reason and purpose in their lives are those who don't fully belong here. They are the serving class, including Malvolio and Feste, and those who come from elsewhere and have imported different and clearer values.

Malvolio becomes the entertainment of the Illyrians; he is the diversion that unites them in antipathy and sympathy which, in this place, are virtually the same thing. Imprisoned and 'mad', Malvolio supplies a clear and immediate focus for all – they have him in common, regardless of where they stand. And their perceptions of him as mad complement each other; Malvolio is the scapegoat they share, their one source of community and commonality. Each comment about him delineates the speaker more fully than it does Malvolio. It confirms the idea of him as a scapegoat, as one into whom are distilled social dissatisfaction and animosity. Malvolio's status as a stranger, as an emotional, religious, social Other in this world makes him an apt choice as a surrogate victim. Girard has noted that in all societies in which ritual human sacrifice is practised, part of the reason for the survival of the society is the choice of a victim from outside the community. 'All sacrificial victims . . . are distinguishable from the nonsacrificeable beings by one essential characteristic: between these victims and the community a crucial social link is missing, so they can be exposed to violence without fear of reprisal. Their death does not automatically entail an act of vengeance.'[13] Malvolio is thus used in the manner of a sacrificial subject, very largely because he is available for such usage in these terms. Of all the characters in the play he is the most alone and friendless and without perceptible roots or ties in any social or political grouping. Granted that his isolation is rather self-imposed, it remains true that of all the characters he is the easiest to scapegoat simply because of his lack of a 'crucial social link' to the community. As his tormentors are quick to grasp, this missing link to their community means a virtual incapacity for revenge. It is this, above all, that makes him so vulnerable, especially when he is imprisoned. There is no chance or hope of anyone coming to his rescue; simply, there is no one who cares sufficiently about him. Even Feste, though he is for most people the play's lasting image and symbol of isolation, has friends amongst the wastrels and even in Viola herself.

The most palpable thing about Malvolio in confinement is his sheer terror. It is this that has made him a frequent object of sympathy to readers and audiences. The terror of darkness and the terror of being misunderstood or being incomprehensible and the flying assertions and counterassertions of sanity and madness, of darkness and light, between Sir Topas and Malvolio add to the fact of Malvolio's helplessness. They also provide a notion of the general helplessness of the lunatic: he can be contradicted by the most palpable untruth or falsehood and remain categorically insane if that is what the sane world wishes.

> *Clown.* Say'st thou that house is dark?
> *Mal.* As hell, Sir Topas.
> *Clown.* Why, it hath bay windows transparent as barricadoes, and the clerestories toward the south north are as lustrous as ebony; and yet complainest thou of obstruction?
> *Mal.* I am not mad, Sir Topas. I say to you this house is dark.
>
> (IV, 2, 32–8)

The audience and reader are put into the position, so frequent in comedy, of siding with the crowd against the individual in his humiliation and degradation. It is the palpability of Malvolio's fear, the real, unexaggerated terror of the confinement of an innocent person unable to prove his innocence, that is so alarming. There is no rational way out of prison for him. He cannot rely on process, on a trial, on being allowed to prove himself wrongly confined. His salvation must be random, unpredictable; it occurs, finally, just because Feste delivers Malvolio's letter to Olivia from the prison. There is, of course, also satisfaction in Malvolio's punishment, such as his humiliating recognition that he needs now to court favour with the very fool whom he once denigrated to his lady. But, in most ways, the torture he is compelled to endure is not a pretty sight.

It does, however, alert us to the way madness can function to serve the polity as a weapon against its enemies. Malvolio has been tricked into acting inappropriately: his sexual fantasies have been conjured into public by the ingenuity of his enemies. This done, his behaviour becomes denominated mad by the established authority, his employer. He is treated thereafter as one who has lost his right to freedom, who has become dangerous to the community and is sentenced to 'treatment' by Olivia:

> Good Maria, let this fellow be look'd to. Where's my cousin Toby? Let some of my people have special care of him. I would not have him miscarry for the half of my dowry.
>
> (III, 4, 55–7)

It is at this moment that Malvolio is rendered harmless and reduced to a common object of pity.

While the argument about the universality of human experience
is not much in favour as a basis for approving a dramatic incident,
there is clearly some way in which the widespread audience and
critical sympathy for Malvolio derives from two rather common
cultural experiences. The dark is, on any rational level, no more
frightening than the light; and terrifying experience belongs no less
to the day than the night. And yet, it is clear that the majority of
people learn in infancy to fear the visible darkness in ways that
cause these fears to settle deeply in the psyche. So, too, the fragile
means by which people understand one another through
language, are constantly threatened in normal experience by the
normal experience of not being understood (by a speaker of
another language, for example) and of being misunderstood. It is
perhaps alarming to consider how greatly our sanity depends
upon our ability to understand why we are not being understood,
or why we are being misunderstood. These experiences are regular
reminders of the extreme fragility of the very means of communica-
tion which we allow ourselves too easily to take for granted. Thus
it is that Malvolio's plight in prison, delightfully funny though it
can be, also strikes fear in the audience and a kind of self-pity in
their hearts. Though Malvolio is not mad, his terror is the terror of
one who fears that he may go mad. His reality is suddenly entirely
his own, unshared by any in the community of which he mis-
takenly regarded himself a part. His darkness is their light, his sense
is their nonsense, and though he asseverates his sanity and reason,
his misery comes from his inability to communicate these to rational fellow creatures. This quite horrible comic scene is a remarkable
anticipation of the plight of Kafka's Joseph K; it dangerously tests
the narrow borders between reason and madness, between ordinary truth and insanity.

Malvolio's final appearance is the conclusive element in the
scapegoating ritual. His return to the scene of celebration only
disturbs its equilibrium with the inundation of rage and pain.
Responding to these, Olivia promises him justice – that is, she
promises redress and balance; indeed she offers him a legitimate
revenge:

Prithee be content.
This practice hath most shrewdly pass'd upon thee;

But when we know the grounds and authors of it,
Thou shalt be both the plaintiff and the judge
Of thine own cause.

(V, 1, 339–43)

For a moment the possibility of restoring Malvolio to the fold is given a chance. This possibility has implications for the ordering of the social formation. For Malvolio's restoration implies also a restoration of the lines of authority and the political conditions that obtained in the beginning. In this case, of course, one of the chief sources of discord will have been retained and supported with all of the ingredients back in place for a repetition of the upheavals that are now almost resolved.

It is intriguing and significant how easily and casually Olivia entirely drops her promise of justice to Malvolio. All it takes is Fabian's confession and assertion that there have been injuries on both sides, and Olivia changes her mind with, 'Alas poor fool, how have they baffled thee!'(357) This statement with its deadly combination of sympathy and contempt is probably the unkindest cut the poor fool, Malvolio, receives in the play. And with it, Malvolio is placed outside of the realm of revenge and justice and transformed into everybody's fool. He is virtually dismissed with Olivia's remark, a public declaration of her sympathy with his tormentors. He is the 'poor fool' and they, therefore, are his betters.

With his last words Malvolio leaves the stage. Ostensibly and apparently he exits freely and of his own volition, but he really has nowhere else to go than away from these people who are in such obvious agreement about him and who have used his foolish vanity to give themselves the pleasure of a common object of merriment and pity. He cannot stay where he is, for he is surrounded by the people who have tormented and humiliated him and by those who, after the discovery, are willing to countenance this treatment.

In *Twelfth Night*, though madness is used as a joke, as a way to reduce someone else to an object of laughter and ineffectuality, we are provided with a vivid glimpse of how the fact of madness is regarded and politicised by the group which it threatens. The process of madness is ingeniously exploited by his enemies, while Malvolio is destroyed very largely by his own efforts. Indeed, the final exit he makes has the appearance of being self-willed and voluntary. And yet that exit has the same force as if he had been banished by a higher power than his own. He is expelled from the garden of comedy and the celebrations are permitted to continue without his souring presence. It is intriguing to observe the extent to which Malvolio's ostensible madness has invalidated him as a valued servant and member of the community. When Olivia first hears of his debility she states 'I would not have him miscarry for the half of my dowry.'(III, 4, 58) His behaviour altogether, however, has seemed so close to madness that concern for his welfare easily gets lost. It is without a show of concern that she allows him to tear angrily away from the group, and it is not difficult to understand that his general threat of revenge includes the mistress who casts him off with such readiness. But such is the power of the idea of madness in this collectivity that its taint cannot be wiped away. Malvolio is forever stigmatized as one who was mad enough to think he could break the barriers of class. Such an indifference to the rigid social stratification which is acknowledged and respected by all other characters is regarded as a sure mark of overweening self-regard which society will easily call crazy, but will not readily forgive.

Notes

1. Christopher Hill, *The World Turned Upside Down: Radical Ideas during the English Revolution*, p. 225.
2. *The World Turned Upside Down*, p. 227.
3. Though King Lear is not locked up until he is an actual prisoner of war, his political ideas of revolution and the redistribution of wealth are potentially dangerous to the ruling class. These ideas are, however, ineffective in the context of his isolation. That isolation ended, he is incarcerated as a danger to the state.
4. *The World Turned Upside Down*, p. 223.
5. Enid Welsford, *The Fool: His Social and Literary History* (Gloucester: Peter Smith, 1966), p. 72.
6. R. D. Laing, *The Politics of Experience* (New York: Pantheon Books, 1967), p. 72.
7. *The Politics of Experience*, p. 35.
8. Anthony Arblaster, *The Rise and Decline of Western Liberalism*. It is usually forgotten that Edmund Burke, the so-called architect of Conservatism was a Whig. Arblaster notes: 'For one thing Burke was extravagantly venerated by many nineteenth-century British liberals,

who clearly did not regard him as simply a conservative. In fact what Burke did was to articulate, for the first time, many of the anti-revolutionary and anti-radical sentiments, which then became the stock-in-trade of respectable liberalism as much as of conservatism in the century that followed.' p. 227.

9. Christopher Hill, *The Century of Revolution* (London: Thomas Nelson, 1961), pp. 168–70.
10. Alexander Leggatt, *Shakespeare's Comedy of Love* (London: Methuen, 1978), p. 244.
11. Rene Girard, *Violence and the Sacred*, translated by Patrick Gregory (Baltimore: The Johns Hopkins University Press, 1977), pp. 77–8.
12. Girard, p. 78.
13. Girard, p. 13.

10

Sexual Rage in *Othello* and *The Winter's Tale*

The politics and culture of sex and sexuality are most vividly exposed when the possibility of sexual jealousy is realized. It is then that the culturally learned and highly valued practice of possessiveness is transferred from object to person, from material to human subject. It is then that the entire mercantile value system which produced sexual and racial subjection, slavery, and systematized capitalism is most severely challenged, its contradiction and weakness most nakedly revealed. By accusing their wives of sexual infidelity, Othello and Leontes give themselves a desperately needed motive for expressing in words the thing their imaginations both love and fear – the image of their wives making love to other men. Thus they transform sexual agony into an instrument of passionate blame and political authority by which they attempt to transcend the limits of their known selves through a kind of narcissistic adventure which enforces an expansion of those selves by actualizing a secret fear. The other man in each case is a potential threat to the sexual security of the hero, being endowed with virtues well known to his wife. Cassio and Polixenes both possess known and demonstrable sex appeal which makes them the more appropriate figures in the fantasies of the jealous husbands. Those fantasies are made more vivid and easy by the fact that Othello and Leontes know and have admired their counterparts, and take their impetuses from intensely precise forms of 'identification with' the men they suspect. A man in the grip of this form of sexual jealousy necessarily and inevitably substitutes the image of his counterpart for his image of himself. The relationship between these two imagined selves takes the form of a transference of known feeling – emotional and physical – to an unexperienced or unknown idea of another. That is, Leontes and Othello are impelled to conceptions of Polixenes and Cassio in postures in which they have not known them, but in which they can imagine them because of their own experience. The transference becomes an erotic fusion of the images of the self and the other. Thus, the initially limited idea of the self is extended not so much by a debasement of that self – a moralistic notion which suggests a narrowing of those limits – but rather by a prising open of the mind through articulated erotic detail. For erotic detail is used in these narratives as a way out of confusion. Sexual passion is given delineational form by a plethora of precisely realized images.

In describing their feelings, the tendency of Othello and Leontes is towards the diminutive. The images of toads and spiders rather than being images of debasement may be seen, in their relative smallness, as attempts towards defining feeling by preciseness. We tend to associate precision with the minuscule. The relation of the human self to that which is small implies an ability to control and contain the object of the relation. A toad in the vapour of a dungeon or a spider in a cup may provoke disgust or fear, but, essential to these details of common life, is the fact of their smallness in relation to the human who observes them. Their smallness allows the human the leisure of contemplating them, fundamentally unthreatened by them. Furthermore, the relation of the observer to the smaller object seems to conform to notions of a hierarchical and patriarchal political structure from which the conceptions issue. The impulse towards control contained in the images encapsulates in a deliberately disgusting or disgusted manner the unchanged power relationship that prevails between the men and women of the plays.

As sexual jealousy grows, it changes its own form as it changes the mind of the man suffering from it. In each play there is a clearly determinable process by which over time the characters reveal the working of this form of feeling. In each play there comes a dynamic moment at which the protagonists suddenly know with dreadful certainty that their wives have betrayed them sexually. From this moment the knowledge of betrayal charges their whole lives until the equally dynamic discovery of their wives' innocence. The first discovery in *Othello* is, of course, slow in coming, and the audience must watch the hero's gradual entrapment by Iago. Leontes, on the other hand, takes the audience entirely by surprise. In a sudden outburst to himself, he reveals that all is wrecked in his life and that he is sure of his wife's infidelity.

In *Othello*, certainty is signalled by the lines, 'She's gone, I am abus'd, and my relief / Must be to loathe her.'(III, 3, 270–1) The sentence comes in the middle point of a speech which begins in

tenuous doubt leading to the assertion. It is the nature of his doubt
that explains the hero's susceptibility which, once articulated, becomes a means towards his confirmation of the *essential* reasonable-
ness of Desdemona's betrayal. In his explanation to himself of
Desdemona's unfaithfulness, Othello acknowledges his wife's superior judgement. He declares himself to be, at least on a social and
sexual level, unfit to be her husband: 'Haply, for I am black, / And
have not those soft parts of conversation / That chamberers have,
or for I am declin'd / Into the vale of years.'(III, 3, 267–270) The
implicit argument of these lines is that she has found him out; that
her clearer judgement has triumphed. The struggle in his mind,
then, is between his knowledge of his unworthiness and an over-
mastering passion for Desdemona. In discussing the contradictory
bases of Othello's jealousy, Stanley Cavell describes the 'structure
of his emotion as he is hauled back and forth across the keel of his
love.'[1] We might note in the speech the opposing characterizations
of the wife who has betrayed him and of himself. Desdemona is a
wild hawk, a haggard, free and flying above, Othello is a toad: 'I
had rather be a toad, / And live upon the vapour of a dungeon, /
Than keep a corner in the thing I love. . . .'(III, 3, 274–6) The
self-perception of the image is, of course, at terrific odds with the
self-perceptions which Othello offers in public, as when he proclaims his own greatness. But their spontaneity argues them to be
more close to the already-perceived self than the self-consciously
extended narrative proclamations about the character Othello
claims himself to be. Those claims, described sometimes as Othello's 'real self'[2] are, however, the unreal and uncertain fictional
public self. The senate speech is a *tour de force* of heroic narrative,
but it has little to do with the self Othello seems really to believe in.
Rather, it is the self he *wants to* believe in. The spontaneous and
private expressions possess greater conviction: the man who sees
and knows himself as old, black, and a stranger, not really capable
of winning the love of the beautiful Venetian virgin, is the other
man Othello thinks he really is.

For Leontes, the certainty of his wife's infidelity comes with a
dynamic suddenness, catching the audience and, more decidedly,
the reader, unawares. In an explosive aside he shows his rage and
exposes his motive:

Too hot, too hot!
To mingle friendship far, is mingling bloods.

I have *tremor cordis* on me: my heart dances,
But not for joy – not joy. This entertainment
May a free face put on, derive a liberty
From heartiness, from bounty, fertile bosom,
And well become the agent: 't may, I grant:
But to be paddling palms, and pinching fingers,
As now they are, and making practis'd smiles
As in a looking glass; and then to sigh, as 'twere
The mort o' th' deer – O, that is entertainment
My bosom likes not, nor my brows.

(I, 2, 108–19)

The *tremor cordis* is a brilliant dramatic stroke: it identifies with wonderful specificity the feelings of Leontes by lending a clinical name to sensation. The feeling is conveyed by the broken, hard-breathed syntax that follows: 'my heart dances, / But not for joy – not joy.' As Othello develops his feelings through a rational process, a careful working out of the reasons for what he senses to be true, Leontes goes in an opposite direction with feeling paramount, reason pursuant. As Othello takes his cue from his outsideness, his social marginality, Leontes is inspired by purely erotic sensation brought on by a kind of visionary voyeurism. Having instructed his wife to play her role as wife / woman – i.e. obedient to his wish and seductive of his friend – he becomes stricken by her success. Carol Thomas Neely has observed that as Leontes speaks, malice erupts 'from beneath the surface of the style; passion does not merely overthrow reason but corrupts it and is incited by it. Leontes' jealousy springs from a pre-rational, pre-linguistic state of consciousness, characterized by its "indeterminacy".'[3] He sends her from him to win his friend by the use of her female art and steps away from them watch her prowess. But he steps away too far, in doing which he places between himself and her a chasm of jealousy. The speech is intensely self-centred, its direction the self-torturing details of pseudo-forensic evidence. Its tension comes from the heavy weight of details stifling the abstractions of friendship and 'not joy'. The details which drive Leontes further into himself are human, personal, precise, and, in a sense, inarguable – they are the tangible facts: heart, face, palms, fingers, smiles, bosom, brows.

Like Othello, Leontes here is seen wrestling with an idea. He is caught by the compulsive human need to interpret what he sees, decoding the evidence of his eyes into terrible visions which the details make real. Leontes actually sees physical contact taking place between Hermione and Polixenes, a sight which makes the imagination of sexual contact a near leap. Howard Felperin has proposed the radical and the deliberately unretractable notion that 'Leontes' jealousy and destructive passion is not quite so flimsy and fanciful, so unfounded . . . as is often casually assumed.' He adds that 'it is impossible to ascertain just what basis there is for Leontes' jealousy. . . . We see enough to know it has some basis, but not enough to say how much.'[4] Iago, on the other hand, has to work entirely upon Othello's mind, for his eyes never offer evidence. Understanding the need for realism, Iago's most brilliantly successful stroke is to postulate Desdemona's infidelity with vivid precision:

> *Iago.* Lie.
> *Oth.*　　　With her?
> *Iago.*　　　　　　　With her, on her, what you will.
> (IV, 1, 33–34)

That slight but devastating substitution of prepositions gives immediate form to the euphemism. The idea becomes a fact. Othello has probably lain on top of Desdemona;[5] he knows what it is like. But his mind is made to see Cassio in the same position. Arthur Kirsch proposes that 'what has clearly become insupportable for Othello in this scene is the fulsomeness of his known sexual instincts and, as his verbal and physical decomposition suggests, his jealous rage against Cassio is ultimately a rage against himself which reaches back to the elemental and destructive triadic fantasies which at one stage in childhood govern the mind of every human being.'[6]

Cassio and Polixenes are, as I have suggested, essential to the 'pleasure' which Othello and Leontes feel and express in their jealous rages. I have described them as possessing sex appeal in the knowledge, of course, that sex appeal is an ideological construction and can mean different things in different contexts and societies. Evidence of male heterosexual sex appeal ultimately derives from the ways in which the character reacts with women. In both *Othello* and *The Winter's Tale* we see Cassio and Leontes with women and are reminded as we watch them of their capacities to relate sexually to women. This discovery, not necessarily a conscious recognition in our reading or seeing the play, is shared by and becomes momentous to the jealous husbands. That is, the men whom they see as rivals are represented as possessing the real potential to be their rivals. Cassio's wit, charm, good looks, and, of course, whiteness are crucial presences in Othello's mind. Polixenes's great similarity to Leontes ('We were as twinn'd lambs that did frisk i' th' sun . . . [I,2,67])[7] explains his dangerousness.

The shock of discovery of female infidelity stems, of course, from a cultural form and contrasts with those cultures which most of us have read about in which the height of masculine hospitality is the sharing of one's wife with a male friend. The response, in each instance, however much a 'learned' one, lies deep in the traditions of each culture and provokes what seem to be powerful 'natural' or 'human' instincts. In each case, however, we must acknowledge that that response is prompted by an ideal of possessiveness. The jealous language of Othello and Leontes reverberates with the phrase 'my wife' in tones of love and hatred. What signifies in the phrase is the juxtaposition of the personal pronoun with the generalized noun. The perceptions of Desdemona and Hermione in their typical roles, and the selves of Othello and Leontes in their individual, strike at the core of the dilemma of jealousy. The treacherous woman has betrayed her function in betraying *me*. Othello, far less than Leontes, is guilty of stereotyping his wife. His greatest distress derives from the compulsive equation of Desdemona's function as wife with her individuality as Desdemona. Leontes, somewhat more solipsistically than Othello, concentrates his jealous rages upon the damage done to himself by her female, wifely, typical act of sexual treachery: 'I have drunk and seen the spider.' ([my emphasis] II,1,45)

King-Kok Cheung has written about the Kierkegaardian notion of dread as an act of recognition of the terrifying imagination of the unimaginable.[8] The act both seduces and frightens the actor, speaking as it does to some appalling desire which society and ethical teaching have declared to be appalling while at the same time, and by implication, urging its possibility. Othello and Leontes are driven to the extremes of passion only by virtue of the discovery of their wives' infidelity, and each almost basks in the illuminations which each extremity of emotion affords. Not capable of a mere acknowledgement of their own jealousy, they seek relief, solace and comfort in their imagination of the horror which the discovery provides. Othello claims that his 'relief must be to loathe her', and yet, instead, his relief derives from self-loathing and self-debasement. Why, we may inquire, *must* Othello's relief be to loathe Desdemona? His words admit of no possible alternative; they argue instead an instinctually understood and unquestioned ideology. It is, of course, Othello's natural-seeming drift to overstatement and social conformity that dictates his response, and it tellingly indicates his passion for imagination.

Not content with the mere abstract notion of infidelity, Othello is subject to powerful mental pictures which more and more discompose him as he sees in imagination the terrifying act occurring. His language indicates a compulsive urge to describe the thing he simultaneously proclaims himself trying to avoid. The attempt to avoid it is, of course, the very thing that gives his mind the ineluctable energy to think the unthinkable. He is trapped by his feeling for Desdemona and as he desires to separate himself from her crime, so his imagination brings him more powerfully close to it:

> What sense had I of her stol'n hours of lust?
> I saw't not, thought it not, it harm'd not me,
> I slept the next night well, was free and merry;
> I found not Cassio's kisses on her lips. . . .

> (III, 3, 344–7)

The language here moves towards the last damning details, obsessively repetitious of his own locus in the triangle, the first-person pronouns proliferate to the climactic moment of vivid specific experience – 'Cassio's kisses on her lips' – from which his presence is excluded. And even in his next speech, Othello's farewell moves away again from the large, the general, the abstract, to the immediately real sexual detail. 'Othello's occupation's gone!' (III, 3, 363), a pun which critics have recognized as both a vocational and a sexual allusion, brings the whole vivid pageant of the great soldier's life back to the real sensual details of a penis and vagina.

Iago's brilliance lies in his perception of the sheer uncontrollability of Othello's sexual imagination, his inability not to flood his mind with pictures both horrible and tempting. Iago's descriptions go as far as they dare but successfully initiate the torrents of ecstatic pain. 'Would you, the supervisor, grossly gape on, / Behold her topp'd?' (III, 3, 401–2) he inquires, with a phrase that contains both the image of Cassio lying on top of Desdemona and, additionally, rings with the sound of the demotic 'tupped' so forcefully employed to disgust Brabantio in Scene One. A few lines later, skillfully narrating the events of the night of Cassio's dream, Iago provides some of the details of Cassio's lustful groaning whereby Othello compulsively implicates his wife.

> And then, sir, would he gripe and wring my hand,
> Cry out, 'Sweet creature!' and then kiss me hard,
> As if he plucked up kisses by the roots,
> That grew upon my lips, then laid his leg
> Over my thigh, and sigh'd, and kiss'd, and then
> Cried 'cursed fate, that gave thee to the Moor!'

(III, 3, 427–432)

;h ideas in their brutal
lds the cruellest detail
hello as 'the Moor' in
to his outsideness, to
o which he has now
ery ready and willing
the dream accurately
:ely reminds him that

ioments deserve close
as being under Iago's
osive and inarticulate
ed as a kind of puppet
hard, though words
l' he cries, 'Death and
sed fate that gave thee
instrous!"' (III, 3, 433)
oon his own request,
il.' (III, 3, 415), upon
iil which then, amaz-
ving reason'.
se, black vengeance,
wed by his expressed
blood!' (458) and 'my

bloody thoughts, with violent pace / Shall ne'er look back . . .'
(463–4)] is a conscious reorganization of the more spontaneously
expressed lust for violent physical contact. These expressions
aggrandize the powerfully *felt* decision to 'tear her all to pieces'
(438) in which the sensual, immediate and concrete mental image
derives force from the urge to plunge his hands into her blood. His
unprovided mind urges him to acts of vengeance which exemplify
a thirst for sexual violence. His need to anatomize his wife, repeated in his threat to 'chop her into messes' (IV, 1, 196), is informed
with sexual connotations in Othello's expressed fear of the power of
her 'body and her beauty' (IV, 1, 201), and given added sexual
strength by his avowed pleasure in the very realism of Iago's plan –
'strangle her in her bed, even the bed she hath contaminated.'
(IV, 1, 203–4) The almost sinister delight Othello takes in the poetic
beauty of the rightness of this exaction savours of sexual excite-
ment. The thoughts the image arouses centre upon the sexuality of
Desdemona, upon the contaminated bed and the lying throat
being circled by his strong hands, the surrender of that body to the
greater power of his own. The context of the decision to murder, of
course, makes it impossible for Othello to separate any act of
Desdemona from the sexual act. His mind is filled up with the
ultimate inseparability of her sexual role from any other she may
try to play; her most innocent remark is seen by him to be related to
her sexual identity. Thus, his response to Iago is an example of
distorted delight because it expresses a reattainment of control of
the sexuality of Desdemona: 'Good, good, the justice of it pleases,
very good.' (IV, 1, 205) The line lingers with its repetitions, its slow
parenthesis, and argues by its pace an inverted but sure perception
by Othello of the possibility of a new kind of happiness born, not
of 'justice', as he claims, but of the renewed control of the sexual
self of the woman he has lost.

Even more obsessively than Othello, Leontes metonymizes his
wife. In a violently aggressive tirade he reduces Hermione to a
vagina. Indeed, his uncharacteristic sexual vocabulary insistently
draws attention to himself and, as events prove, has nothing at all
to do with the subject of his raving except as she has been transformed by his uncontrollable imagination:

> There have been,
> (Or I am much deceiv'd) cuckolds ere now,
> And many a man there is (even at this present,

Now, while I speak this) holds his wife by th' arm
That little thinks she has been sluic'd in's absence
And his pond fish'd by his next neighbour, by
Sir Smile, his neighbour: nay there's comfort in't
Whiles other men have gates, and those gates open'd,
As mine, against their will . . . be it concluded,
No barricado for a belly.

(I, 2, 190–204)

The harsh demotic euphemisms in this speech are a means to relief. Leontes' concentrated use of obscenity consists in obsessive variations on the idea and image of sexual organs. The speech takes its energy from the implications of 'sluic'd', 'pond fish'd', 'gates', 'belly'. As Othello sought relief through loathing, so Leontes here describes himself as deriving comfort from the commonness of his lot. This is, of course, a palpable self-deception. His comfort comes not from the fact that other men have unfaithful wives but, instead, that femaleness is a moral concept, that women betray men and lie. His images are significant indicators of the attempt to simplify the sexual relationship of men and women and to reduce it to a controllable proportion. Is it more possible for Leontes than for the reader to refrain from being directed by words like 'sluic'd' and 'fish'd' in the present context towards the imagination of a purely sexual act between a man and a woman? And do not these words possess pornographic connotations whereby the image specifically intends to reduce the woman to her sexual function? And, finally, is there not in the intention of this reduction a kind of pleasure denoted in the speaker's discovery of the simple 'truth'?

Like Othello, Leontes reveals simply that he possesses a pornographic imagination. His language, which some critics like to refer to as tainted, shows him almost incapable of seeing Hermione as more or less than a vagina. However much he tries to refer to her in terms of himself and themselves, the vocabulary which keeps driving to the surface of his speech is that of sexual abuse; the language he uses that of passionate obsession. Felperin proposes, on the contrary, 'Leontes' suspicion of the word', a suspicion that 'thrives upon verbal mannerism, sophistication, even preciosity that dominates the language of Sicilia from the play's initial dialogue, and that works to obscure as much as it reveals.'[9]

It is surely noteworthy that until he reveals his jealousy, Leontes is a relatively silent character displaying little of himself except a rather laconic, stolid side. The speakers and self-revealers in scene ii are Polixenes and Hermione. Their speeches denote their senses of freedom, ease, and pleasure, as each of them finds expression simple and untense. The longest speech Leontes utters in this early part of the scene is the four-line description of his courtship of Hermione and his winning of her 'white hand' (I, 2, 102). In addition, as Neely notes, 'Leontes depersonalizes Hermione and Polixenes from the moment jealousy emerges. . . . He scarcely calls them by name again [after I, 2, 109] in the first act.'[10] By contrast, Polixenes and Hermione make speeches more than twice this length quite frequently in response to the slightly mordant challenges and questions of Leontes, whose very silence in the context of their garrulousness exhibits a considerable control of the direction of the action. Thus, when Leontes finally does reveal himself, it is through his language of sexual jealousy. To talk, then, as so many critics have done, of his debasement, is to invert the chronology of the play. He is debased by sexual jealousy only in comparison to the self he reveals after the discovery of Hermione's and Polixenes' innocence. His previous self is unknown except through palpably flattering references to it by his wife and friend; to a spirit within him of which there is no evidence until after he has undergone the transforming suffering of guilt.

Both Othello and Leontes express their jealousy in part through the agencies of abuse and name-calling. As I have said, much of the abuse of each of these characters has the explicit function of describing their wives in vaginal terms. When Leontes asks, 'Ha' not you seen, Camillo . . . my wife is slippery?' (I, 2, 268–74) he is, I think, obliquely referring to her vagina – to sexual secretions – deriving a kind of masochistic pleasure from the charged, textured, word 'slippery'. I wonder if this reading of the word is not widely shared, though it is not much written about. Eric Partridge enters this use of slippery as an example of bawdy, while he avoids saying precisely why it is bawdy with the following euphemistic explanation: 'The semantics may perhaps be explained by *greasy* or by the fact that Leontes thinks that she is preparing to slip from virtue to infidelity.'[11] But, of course, Leontes is already certain that she has slipped from virtue to infidelity and is here using the adjective as a means of reducing his wife to something less than a wife, in perfect accord with the harsh sexually anatomizing language that is his mode up to now. The gross remark is consistent with such subsequent abuse of Hermione as a 'bed swerver' (II, 1, 93) and the agonized reference to bed sheets, 'which, being spotted / Is goads, thorns, nettles, tails of wasps'. (I, 2, 327–8)

But no words he speaks as violently and deliberately intend to debase Hermione as the speech in which Leontes appears almost to be trying to efface his wife's very existence:

> is this nothing?
> Why then the world, and all that's in't, is nothing,
> The covering sky is nothing, Bohemia nothing,
> My wife is nothing, nor nothing have these nothings,
> If this be nothing.

> (I, 2, 292–6)

The evil of the world is distilled into the single idea of female sexual infidelity, a concentration which provides Leontes with a mad impetus. The force and energy of his passion almost overwhelm his power of speech as he seems to be on the verge of losing the ability to articulate in the driving and explosively repeated word *nothing*. This word seems to present itself unavoidably, try as he might to circumvent it, with his desperate plunging in other directions. An actor trying to give meaning to these lines might pause before each of the first four *nothings* as a way of suggesting that Leontes is seeking a way out of this obsession, but, with the repetition of the word, conceding his failure to do so.

Terry Eagleton reminds us that 'nothing' is an Elizabethan euphemism for the vagina. With some overstatement, he perceptively notes that the 'woman's nothing is of a peculiarly convoluted kind, a yawning abyss within which man can lose his virile identity.'[12] Harriet Hawkins has warned us that we 'can't count to ten without thinking of a rabbit.'[13] And the force of the joke applies here. Leontes, aggressively and obsessively thinking of Hermione as a sexual entity, is himself as caught by the pun or euphemism as those who hear him. *Nothing* is not merely an absence of matter, it is the material evidence of femaleness, and it is this aspect of femaleness which has come to dominate his vision of the whole world. The intimations of nihilism in this speech, the passionately destructive energy which it unleashes, are given weight and conviction by the presence of the ironic countermeaning of the repeated word.

As Leontes turns his attack on Camillo, five lines later, he reveals the form of the tortuous pleasure he derives from abuse:

> It is: you lie, you lie:
> I say thou liest, Camillo, and I hate thee.

(I, 2, 299–300)

Again he repeats a word which defines not merely the 'other' but which demonstrates a method of deriving consolation and warped pleasure. One of the functions of abuse, in evidence here certainly, and in *Othello*, is to increase the distance between the abuser and the object of his abuse. By degrading another through namecalling, the self is exalted. Obviously a direct relationship is established between the abuser and the abused – at least in the mind of the abuser – through a symbiosis established by language. By describing Hermione as *nothing*, Leontes is effectively describing himself; and, of course, her innocence of his charges makes the process of self-definition the more palpable to the reader. Shakespeare offers here, more even than in *Othello*, an entire drama staged within the mind of a character, a drama which, while unreal and insubstantial, utterly transforms the world he inhabits. The transformation is accomplished through an implicit narrative of his own creating. This is a story of which he is the hero, a wronged innocent, gulled and betrayed by the evil of others. His apprehension of his relation to the act of infidelity is nowhere so tellingly discovered as when, with the voice of deep relief, he recognizes in Polixenes' hasty departure the vindication of his suspicions with the strange exclamation, 'How blest am I / In my just censure!' (II, 1, 35–6) In the single word 'blest' is concentrated a perverse fulfillment of his wishes. The word is, surely, exactly the wrong one in the context; yet, though oddly out of place, its presence signifies a sense of almost spiritual achievement. His abuse of those around him is a way of asserting the absoluteness of his own innocence and the criminality and evil of the world in which he himself is an offending part. The reduction, then, of others to one-dimensional elements of that world, to things and pieces and immoral components of it, is a form of passionate asseveration of his moral distance from it. Leontes is acting from a need for which his imagination provides the pretext and circumstances the context. That need seems to be the transcendent pleasure of relief. Othello, very much unlike him, falls into the hands of another narrator than himself, one who takes captive his imagination and directs its motions.

Both Leontes and Othello are drawn by self-torturing voyeurism to the details of their wives' infidelity. Each hero is fascinated by his own reaction to the abhorrent idea; and each makes the idea more fascinating by making it seem more real by fleshing it out with terrible precision. Both are obsessed with the human body and both give their obsessions the form of reality by translating them into their specific component parts. Sexual fantasies, as readers of sex literature know, depend largely upon the realization of a sexual act through the inclusion of detail in the narrative. Without sexual detail, the pornography is mere romance, feeding the imagination with outlines for the mind to colour in.

Othello's so-called 'brothel scene' is a similar attempt by the hero to regain his status by abuse. It has often been noted that in this scene Othello treats Desdemona as though she were a prostitute, with the implication that it is all right to treat a prostitute in this appalling way but not a chaste wife. The justification implied by this reading of Othello's treatment of his wife is that Iago has led him to it and that Othello is an innocent victim of the play's villain. But, if we can free ourselves from the ideological concomitants of the unequal treatment of *kinds* or categories of women which this reading takes for granted, we may more easily be able to see what Othello is doing to himself in the scene. In his language he reveals what he believes to be the worst thing a woman can be: he has discovered the word by which to stereotype and brand his wife. He has discovered that the means to relief is to excise utterly those parts of herself which he has not hated and to concentrate his whole knowledge of her on the part he fears. The sexual obsession of Othello, ripened into direct language – 'for foul toads / To knot and gender in!' (IV, 2 , 63–4) – is most powerful in his abuse of Desdemona as a whore and strumpet, and gains force by virtue of his repetition of the crude but wholly defining words. He has found her out; she is the 'cunning whore of Venice' (IV, 2, 91) and he is again Othello the warrior hero – not Othello the husband of Desdemona. That is, the abuse he vents upon his wife is a means of separating himself from her, of reconstituting the innocent

Othello, gulled, perhaps, by a wily woman like so many other men; Othello the hero who knows a whore when he sees one and who knows how to treat a whore.

Unwittingly, of course, Desdemona plays into Othello's hands by using the language her husband deems appropriate to a treacherous whore, invoking heaven and her faith to bear witness to her truth. These expostulations are meat and drink to the manly warrior who displays a genuine relish in uncovering his wife's deception. His sarcastic speech, whose bitterness is expressive of a new distance between them, demonstrates a histrionic, if tortured delight:

> I cry you mercy,
> I took you for that cunning whore of Venice,
> That married with Othello: you mistress,
> That have the office opposite to Saint Peter
> And keeps the gates in hell, ay, you, you, you!
> We ha' done our course; there's money for your pains
> I pray you turn the key, and keep our counsel.

(IV, 2, 90–6)

The sarcasm he employs in this speech denotes a control which is a far cry from the ravaging self-pity of his earlier Job-echoing speech in which he talks only of himself. Now that he has discovered another subject than himself – Desdemona, his opposite, his betrayer – he rises to a different kind of eloquence. Othello, in this passage, is suddenly not 'I' or 'me', but 'Othello', that ironically observed character who plays a part in the narrative he here relates. The offer of money is a sudden conflation of 'Othello' and himself, of narrative and life; as a self-dramatizing and artful *act* it seems to possess not a little of self-congratulation.

In each of the plays, the perception of their wives' infidelity initiates a process of adaptation to the 'fact'. Initially, the discovery creates moral and emotional confusion in Leontes and Othello. Each character thinks he has discovered an evil act, yet each reacts to the discovery with a certain amount of ambivalence which partially meliorates the evil. Othello's desire to kill his wife takes the form of truly bloody and blood-thirsty sexual desire. The raging and fuming which accompany his menace are informed with a horrible spontaneous lust for violent physical contact with Desdemona. And, notwithstanding the absurd pieties of the 'It is the cause' speech, it is with fierce physical abuse that Othello finally stifles his wife. Cavell has pointed to the way 'Othello's mind continuously outstrips reality, dissolves it in trance or dream,'[14] a notion which explains how the motions of this speech transform it into an astonishing self-deluding homage to rationality and bourgeois morality. The whole, so lush with the famous 'Othello music', is an extended rationalization of murder which derives its central argument from a huge self-aggrandizing lie. The logic of 'Yet she must die, else she'll betray more men' (V, 2, 6) is that Othello is about to murder his wife lest she do to Cassio's successors in her bed what she has done to Othello himself. The words are Othello's, the idea is his, and it seems to me that to try to make something beautiful out of them, though undoubtedly they are constructed out of words and images which cultural convention declares to be 'beautiful', is to remove the very centre of the construction. Shakespeare himself seems to have recognized the fraudulence of the sacrifice Othello is here trying to perform by having Desdemona awaken and by making, finally, not a murder out of a sacrifice but a murder out of a murder, refusing dramatically, logically, or linguistically, to allow the distinction. The speech, deservedly famous, is a fascinating example of sensual self-pleasuring. Othello's decision to kill his wife beautifully has brought back to him the absolute control over her body which he had felt to be lost. He sees, smells, and feels Desdemona; he satiates himself upon her living presence. Marianne Novy remarks that 'the more he imagines her guilt, the more he feels his own attraction to her. . . . He plans to kill her as a way to control his own unruly passion for her body as he punishes himself.'[15]

Leontes too seems driven by an impulse to regain control through sacrifice. Several times he speaks of destroying Hermione by fire as if to efface her through a rite of purification:

> say that she were gone,
> Given to the fire, a moiety of my rest
> Might come to me again.

(II, 3, 7–9)

The desire for relief through destruction is here, as in *Othello*, a logical consequence of the foaming sexual fury which manifested itself in imagined details. Here too, the murderous impulse is more controlled, aggrandized by reference to self-justification: rest, relief, and social order will be achieved by sacrifice. Each hero, then, seems to have reconstituted his sexual pleasure in the idea of his wife's infidelity, to have restored his sanity by a resolution of his fragmented imagination. The process of anatomization has found an acceptable expression, the details of her infidelity have been resolved into a larger scheme which accords with the ethos of the world each inhabits.

Notes

1. Stanley Cavell, *The Claim of Reason: Wittgenstein, Skepticism, Morality and Tragedy* (Oxford, Clarendon Press: 1979), p. 484.
2. Giorgio Melchiori, 'The Rhetoric of Character Construction: *Othello*.' *Shakespeare Survey: 35* (Cambridge: Cambridge University Press, 1982), p. 66.
3. Carol Thomas Neely, '*The Winter's Tale*: The Triumph of Speech,' *SEL* 15(1975), p. 324.
4. Howard Felperin, '"Tongue-tied our queen?"': the deconstruction of presence in *The Winter's Tale*,' *Shakespeare and the Question of Theory*, ed. Patricia Parker and Geoffrey Hartman (New York: Methuen, 1985), p. 7.
5. Eric Partridge notes that in Shakespeare 'the man is always on top.' *Shakespeare's Bawdy* (New York: E. P. Dutton, 1960), p. 48.
6. Arthur Kirsch, 'The Polarization of Erotic Love in *Othello*', *MLR* 73(1978), 737.
7. Coppelia Kahn writes of this passage that it indicates that Leontes sees Polixenes as his double; that it implies a homosexual fantasy, and that it indicates Leontes' desire to escape his mature sexuality. *Man's Estate* (Berkeley: University of California Press, 1981), p. 215.
8. King-Kok Cheung, 'Shakespeare and Kierkegaard: Dread in *Macbeth*.' *Shakespeare Quarterly* 35, 4 (Winter, 1984), pp. 430–440.
9. Felperin, p. 10.
10. Neely, p. 327.
11. *Shakespeare's Bawdy*, p. 189.
12. Terry Eagleton, *William Shakespeare* (Oxford: Basil Blackwell, 1986), p. 64.
13. Harriet Hawkins, *Likenesses of Truth in Elizabethan and Restoration Drama* (Oxford: Clarendon Press, 1972), p. 60.
14. Cavell, p. 484.
15. Marianne Novy, *Love's Argument: Gender Relations in Shakespeare* (Chapel Hill: University of North Carolina Press, 1984), p. 138.

Index